*Approaching the Qur'an for the beginner i.
mixture of wisdom intended locally for the
appropriate for all times and places. The sourc
both, the application different.*

*One usually recommends beginning with the Meccan surah's and verses, those
revealed the earliest. These unveil a simple, universal message. Look to nature
for the "verses" of the divine book. We don't live in these forms forever: we come
from somewhere and are heading back to the same source. We are responsible for
our actions, the results of which will always turn up. Therefore, caution about the
human ego, acting justly towards others and constantly checking-in with the Source
beyond time and space are all part of the original human "user's guide."*

– Dr Neil Douglas-Klotz, author of
The Sufi Book of Life and A Little Book of Sufi Stories

إِنَّ هَٰذَا ٱلْقُرْءَانَ يَهْدِى لِلَّتِى هِىَ أَقْوَمُ وَيُبَشِّرُ ٱلْمُؤْمِنِينَ ٱلَّذِينَ يَعْمَلُونَ ٱلصَّٰلِحَٰتِ أَنَّ لَهُمْ
أَجْرًا كَبِيرًا ﴿٩﴾

*Indeed, this Qur'an guides to that which is most upright and gives good tidings to the
trusting who do righteous deeds that they will have a great reward. [17:9]*

*The Qur'an is the revealed knowledge and light that encompasses the patterns,
meanings, and purpose of existence. This book presents Qur'anic Universal
renderings that connects the absolute and the relative in a unified voice that
transforms and transports the reader to the eternal reality that is both transcendent
and immanent. It is an essential reference for the inner technology guiding towards
transformation that echoes in the hearts of the sincere seeker. It can be an effulgent
light, and a source of guidance for the illumined human being that aspires to a
vision of reality where Allah's Attributes are seen in everything and in every
situation, realizing that he is truly witnessing his creator as evident in everything
that exists by His grace.*

– Adnan al Adnani, author of
Lights of Consciousness: A Sufi view of Science and Spirituality

UNIVERSAL QUR'AN

- Selected Verses for all Times -

Shaykh Fadhlalla Haeri

Zahra Publications

Zahra Publications

ISBN: 978-1-928329-21-3
eISBN: 978-1-928329-22-0
Published by Zahra Publications
Distributed and Published by Zahra Publications
PO Box 50764
Wierda Park 0149 Centurion
South Africa
www.zahrapublications.pub
www.zahrapublications.com

Designed and typeset in South Africa by Quintessence Publishing
Cover Design by Quintessence Publishing
Project Management by Quintessence Publishing

Set in 11 point on 14 point, Garamond

Table of Contents

Editorial Note

I have always believed that the message of the Qur'an is universal and useful at all times and for all people. This belief motivated me to select the verses that are clearly universal always. As a result of this intent, I took the liberty of rendering the meanings of the verses in an easily accessible way to the modern reader, rather than trying to adhere to a classically acceptable translation. The verses selected are **_renderings_** of the inner meaning, rather than a traditional translation.

This selection of verses came about during the course of another book project, which encompasses a Sufi Reflection on the Qur'an. In that process, it became clear that the present needs of human beings in this day and age, require more reference to the Source of creation, and Divine Light – which are largely Meccan verses, and which this book presents a selection of.

The selected verses help with personal transformation and the rise in consciousness and Universal Truth, rather than with relationship, community, law and other aspects of conduct.

In order to make these verses easily accessible to the modern reader, I tried to neutralise the impact of any cultural or historical aspects in language occasionally summarised in some places and highlighted in other places. This was done in only a few verses, to bring focus to the sincere seekers attention. This liberty was taken for that impact only.

We are living at an age where suffering, sorrow and anger are universally afflicting human beings. The only way out of this misery and darkness is to connect with the light of the Qur'an and internalise it, by excluding all other mental distractions and agitations. This is the age where we need regular spiritual recharge and awakening to the truth within our hearts.

Shaykh Fadhlalla Haeri
July 2020

Acknowledgements

Over a number of years several people have assisted in bringing this compilation together. I would like to thank firstly the team of translators who had made available the initial renderings of these verses. They have been dedicatedly working with me on a forthcoming publication that will encompass the whole Qur'an. For the purpose of this special selection of verses, guided by the thread of the Qur'an's universal message, I thank Hashim Ismail, Fatima Laher, Yusuf Muslim, Andrew Tudhope and Ahmed Baasith Sheriff for assisting in the editing and reviewing; Muna Bilgrami, Abbas Bilgrami, Leyya Kalla, Aliya Batul Haeri, Hasnayn Ebrahim's and Mohamed Bulbulia for the arrangement and supervision of this book.

Introduction

The human story is the ultimate challenge to every contemplative person. At one time or another each of us wonders about the meaning and purpose of life and where it will end. From the evidence of many thousands of years, our prehistoric ancestors were also obsessed with this question. We now also have archaeological evidence suggesting that the issue of the origin of life and death; the hereafter; our relationship with God; the extent to which humans were given freedom to act; and our real responsibility on earth, are all essential concerns in our past, present and without a doubt will continue to be so in the future.

From the early days of agricultural settlements a few thousand years ago, certain individuals who had a greater intuitive capacity to relate the past to the present and future were considered important beings in their communities and cultures. As humans evolved along the natural arc of evolution towards a better understanding of natural events and greater exposure to different levels of consciousness, world religions emerged through great prophets and seers, influencing human progress. Religions have served humanity by providing stability and ethical values which helped the early emerging settlements and communities to bond firmly and gave them a better chance of survival. The natural drive in human beings is to acquire power and enforce the path towards higher consciousness and a better quality of life.

Over the past few centuries the human project has gravitated towards material progress and development. These have been important to bring about improvements in the visible aspects of life. Access to the records of recent history, as well as those which are much older, show us clearly that basic human contentment relates to shelter, health, food and quality social connectedness. After fulfilling our basic survival needs, we seek intrinsic, long-lasting inner contentment which the great prophets had addressed and emphasised.

The Abrahamic traditions were the result of thousands of prophets and messengers and culminated with the Prophet Muhammad, whose gift of the Qur'an is of universal value. The message of the Qur'an does not contradict other world religions or spiritual paths. The modern world we are living in where race, culture, religion and all other characteristics can meet, connect and fuse, presents so many challenges regarding faith, belief and all other metaphysical issues. The amazing Qur'an can shed helpful light on these dynamics.

The book in your hand is an attempt to present key verses which are universally useful at all times and for all people. They are presented in an order that may help to address key issues in the human journey. The Qur'an's miracle is that it repeatedly connects the infinite unseen cosmic lights with the finite, relative, and limited earthly consciousness. The seamless connection between heavenly powers and the earthly limitations are shown repeatedly.

Our experiences of life are bound by space and time with a personal identity and biography which is bracketed between birth and death. The mystery of life is that it is both cosmic and boundless and yet experienced within space and time by everyone. The ultimate human challenge is to realise that personal life is inseparable from perpetual life itself. The Divine Cosmic Light is in every heart and it is that which leads the reflective individual to experience the inseparability of personal life and infinite life itself. That is where humanity and divinity dwell together.

When the human project is understood mentally and accepted by the heart, a true understanding of this seamless connection between God and man or the Absolute and the relative will illumine us. If this book is approached with humility, trust and faith, it can bring about a real change in the attitude towards oneself, other human beings, and life itself.

For the Qur'an to make an impact on your life, you must under-stand and take into account the culture of the day the Arabic language was very different from our culture and languages of today. The early Muslims lived in an environment hostile to survival; fear and sorrow were the most dominant emotions of that time. Nowadays, our concerns for survival are reduced and our hopes point toward higher consciousness and the experience of what is behind the limitations of space and time.

There are countless ways of awakening to the truth. One clear way is to come to know that personal life is only a spark from cosmic life, and cosmic life is perpetual. When you know that your soul is eternal then your attitude towards day to day existence will change radically. You may live the moment intensely as if it is forever and at the same time you can care for the limited reality that we humans experience within space and time, which we call normal consciousness. If you imbibe the meanings of these verses, then you will come to know that conditioned consciousness, with all its challenges and frustrations, is a prelude to cosmic consciousness which is the origin of limited human consciousness as well as its destiny. To honour life fully we must accept our primal duty of dealing with dualities and pluralities whilst striving to see the connectivity with the ever-prevailing Unity. The blessing that we are caught in duality enables us to progress along the lights that ultimately lead to the intense divine light of absolute Oneness.

It is through true honesty and the courage to face the state you are in that will propel you to attain the purpose and duty of your life. The ultimate state of well-beingness is that you acknowledge the lower self, the ego and all the tricks of the mind, whilst calibrating all the while with your soul or spirit which consistently reflects Truth. In reality, we own nothing and control nothing except for the tiniest of portions, which enable us to interact with the world outside as best we can. Every one of us is both local and universal. The ultimate grace upon all human beings is to be able to think, evaluate, be rational and yet to also go beyond that to the zone of the perfect and eternal soul or spirit within.

For this reason we can evaluate the goodness of human beings by their deeds and way of life: what is most desirable and durable as far as all humanity is concerned. These verses will help you to focus and flow along Cosmic Grace. The ultimate truth will become clear to everyone when the soul leaves the body and mind on earth and ascends back to its heavenly domain. To transcend the earthly limitations is the best preparation for the feared experience of death and the hereafter.

I: Life Eternal - Appearing in Cycles

From prehistoric times, human beings have wondered about the origin of life, its purpose and meaning, and what happens in death and after it. With a few thousand years of reflection and sharing between different people and cultures, we now have some basis to shine light upon this key puzzle and challenge. One theistic outcome is that there is One Cosmic Light from which countless energies, transmissions, and radiations emanate throughout the universe.

Human life on earth is based on conflicting, as well as complementary, dualities and pluralities. The biggest force in human life is to connect, understand, and know the real nature of events, as well as the physical, biological and emotional activities taking place within us. The drive to maintain continuity and transcend the limitations of space and time indicate that the truth of life itself is eternal in nature and boundless, even if it appears transient in the form of human life.

Every event in the universe has a beginning and an end. Individual human life follows this rule. Yet every intelligent person wishes to know what is beyond the natural boundaries of space and time. Few people have experienced a state that transcends space and time. Many have experienced near death, out of body, or other unusual paranormal states. Real prophetic revelations confirm the inseparability of the absolute and the relative. God permeates the universe and thus governs and controls all, except the very limited power of choice that is given to human beings and to other living entities, both known and unknown, such as the jinn and angels.

A. Unique Cosmic Light

67:1 Holds Power over Everything

Blessed is He in Whose hand is sovereignty, who holds power over all things.

59:24 Whose Attributes are Desired by All Creation

He is God, the Creator, the Originator, the Shaper. The best names belong to Him. Everything in the heavens and earth glorifies Him. He is the Almighty, the Wise.

39:62 The Creator and Master of All

God is the Creator of all things, the Guardian of all things.

40:68 The Source of Eternal Life, Cycles of Life and Death

It is He Who gives life and causes it to die, and when He decrees a thing, He but says to it 'Be,' and it is.

3:6 Causing Appearance

It is He Who shapes you all in the womb as He pleases. There is no God but Him, the Mighty, the Wise.

3:109 Whatever is Known and Unknown Emanates from Divine Light

To Allah belongs all that is in the heavens and on earth. And to Allah all matters shall revert.

3:129 Mastery

To God belongs what is in the heavens and on earth. He forgives whomsoever He wills and He torments whomsoever He wills. God is All-Forgiving, Compassionate to each.

3:160 God's Power Overcomes All

If God helps you, no one can overcome you; if He forsakes you, who else can help you? Believers should put their trust in Allah.

3:189 The Sovereign of the Universe

To Allah belongs the Kingdom of the heavens and of the earth; and Allah is powerful over everything.

4:132-133 Allah's Purpose is to Be Worshipped

To Allah belongs what is in the heavens and what is on earth, and Allah suffices as All-Worthy of trust. If He so willed, He could remove you altogether and replace you with new people. He has full power to do so.

7:128 Awareness of God

Moses said to his people: 'Turn to Allah for help and be steadfast: the earth belongs to Allah – He gives it as their own to whichever of His servants He chooses and the happy future belongs to those who are conscious of Him.'

4:126 God Encompasses All

To Allah belongs what is in the heavens and what is on earth. God encompasses all things.

10:65 Divine Attributes

The glory belongs altogether to Allah; He is the All-Hearing, the All-Knowing.

10:61 Everything Known to God

...There does not escape your Lord an atom's weight on earth or in heaven, nor smaller than this, nor bigger, except it be in a Manifest Book.

11:6 Perfect Master

There is not a creature that moves on earth whose provision is not His concern. He knows where it lives and its resting place: it is all in a clear Book.

11:123 Be Obsessed with Allah's Might

To Allah belongs the unseen in the heavens and earth. To Him all matters revert. worship Him, trust in Him; nor is your Lord heedless of what you do.

16:1-4 Divine Spirit

…Glory be to Him! High is He, exalted above anything they associate with Him! He sends down the angels with the Spirit of His command… He created the heavens and the earth with the truth.

22:74 Beyond Measure

They do not measure Allah with His true measure; surely God is All-Powerful, Almighty.

23:84-85 Remembrance of Origin

Say: 'To whom does the earth and all upon it belong, if you happen to know?' They will say: 'Allah Say: Will you not then remember?'

37:95-96 Warning

He said: 'Do you worship that which you produce, when it is Allah Who created you and all that you do?'

37:180-182 Glory

Glory be to your Lord, the Lord of Glory, above what they describe! Peace be upon the messengers! Praise be to Allah, Lord of the Worlds.

39:67 Cosmic Dominion

They do not measure God with His true measure. The earth altogether shall be in His grip on the Day of Resurrection...

2:115 The Universe is in the Divine Web

And to God belongs the east and the west. So wherever you turn, there is the Face of God; God is All-Encompassing and Knowing.

24:64 Knowledge Expresses Connectedness and God is the Source of All Connections

To God belongs what is in the heavens and on earth. He knows what you are about, and on the Day they are returned to Him, He shall inform them of what they did. And Allah has knowledge of all things.

28:88 Eternal Light

All things perish, except His Face. His is the Judgment and unto Him you shall be returned.

30:40 One Source

It is Allah Who created you, then provides for you, then causes you to die, then resurrects you. Are any of your partners capable of any of this? Glory to Him! May He be exalted above what they associate with Him!

48:14 Grace

To God belongs sovereignty of the heavens and earth. He forgives whom He wills and punishes whom He wills. God is All-Forgiving, Compassionate to each.

51:51 All Dualities are Manifestations of Unity

...and do not set up any other god alongside Allah. I am sent by Him to give you clear warning!

53:42-49 Destiny of Hereafter

And to your Lord is the destination; and that it is He Who causes laughter and weeping; and that is He Who brings about death and life; and that He creates the pairs, male and female, from a sperm drop, when discharged; and that it is He Who shall undertake the Second Creation; and that it is He Who gives wealth and possessions; and that it is He Who is the Lord of Sirius.

57:5-6 All Within the Divine Web

To Him belongs sovereignty of the heavens and earth, and to Allah all matters shall revert. He makes night merge into day and day into night. He knows what is in every heart.

2:255 Ever-Living, Eternal Power

God, there is no deity save Him, the Ever-Living, the Self-Subsisting. Neither slumber overtakes Him, nor sleep. His is all that is in the heavens and all that is on earth... He knows all that lies open before men and all that lies hidden from them. His eternal power overspreads the heavens and the earth. And He alone is truly Exalted, Tremendous.

B.   Dualities & Pluralities Expressing Unity

1:1 Reference and Permission

In the name of God, the Merciful to all, the Compassionate to each!

55:1-4 Cosmic Mercy and Evident Compassion

The All-Merciful! He taught the Qur'an. He created man. He taught him eloquence.

16:18 Countless Blessings

If you were to count God's blessings, you could not take stock of them. Allah is All-Forgiving, Compassionate to each.

7:156 To Experience Mercy

He said: 'My torment I inflict upon whomsoever I wish; and My mercy encompasses all things. I shall inscribe My mercy for those who are pious, those who give charity, and those who believe in Our signs.'

42:19 Special Grace

Allah is All-Gentle to His servants, providing for whomsoever He wills. He is the All-Strong, the Almighty.

42:27 Grace and Divine Justice

Had Allah spread out His bounty to His servants, they would have grown shameless on earth. Rather, He dispenses it in any measure He wills. Regarding His servants, He is All-Experienced, All-Seeing.

2:245 The Bounty of Full Surrender

Who will give God a good loan, which He will increase for him many times over? It is Allah who withholds and Allah who gives abundantly, and it is to Him that you will return.

16:71 Earthly Differentiation Hides Soul's Sameness

God has preferred some of you over others in provision, but those granted preference will not turn over their provision to their bondsmen, so as to share it in equity. Do they repudiate the blessings of God?

2:261 Grace of Abundance Due to Generosity

The parable of those who spend their possessions in the way of God is that of a grain out of which grows seven ears, in every ear a hundred grains: for God multiplies unto whom He wills; and God is Infinite, All-Knowing.

39:52-54 Mercy Through Surrender

Do they not know that God spreads out His bounty to whomever He wills and withholds it? In this are signs for a people who have faith. Say: 'O My servants who have transgressed against themselves, do not despair of God's mercy. God forgives all sins: He is All-Forgiving, Compassionate to each. Turn to your Lord and surrender to Him, before the chastisement comes upon you, then you will not be helped.'

4:175 Path of the Believers

Allah will admit those who believe in Him and hold fast to Him into His mercy and favour; He will guide them towards Him on a straight path.

24:55 Prophetic Path

Allah has promised those among you who believe and do righteous deeds that He will make them inherit the earth, as He caused those before them to inherit… and to instil peace of mind….

21:105-107 Worthy Inheritors

In the Psalms We wrote, following the Remembrance, that the earth shall be inherited by my righteous servants. In this is admonition enough for a people of true worship. And We have not sent you but as a mercy to the worlds.

5:65 Belief and Awareness

If only the People of the Book would believe and be cautiously aware of Allah, We would take away their misdeeds and bring them into the Gardens of bliss.

8:29 Forgiveness

Believers, if you remain cautiously aware of God, He will give you a discrimination and wipe out your bad deeds, and forgive you; Allah's favour is great indeed.

64:17 Grace Due to Charity

If you make a generous loan to God, He will multiply it for you and forgive you. God is Ever-Thankful and Forbearing.

6:160 A Good Deed Multiplies Tenfold, a Bad Deed Brings its Equal

A good deed shall have the like of it tenfold; an evil deed shall only be recompensed the like of it...

14:34 Boundless Bounties

And He gives you all that you ask Him; were you to count the bounties of Allah, you could not take stock of them. Mankind is indeed wicked and most ungrateful.

3:8 Prayers for Guidance

'Our Lord, do not let our hearts deviate after You have guided us. Grant us Your mercy. You are the Ever-Giving.'

27:62 The One Giver of All

Is it not He Who answers the one in need when he prays to Him, Who draws away evil and makes you successors in the earth? Is there to be another god with God? Little do you remember!

28:5 Virtue of Humbleness

We, however, wish to bestow Our favour on those held to be weak on earth. We intend to make them leaders to mankind, and make them the inheritors.

31:20 Knowledge of the One Necessary

Have you not seen how Allah has subjected to you whatsoever is in the heavens and earth, and He has lavished on you His blessings, outward and inward? And among men are those that dispute concerning God without knowledge or guidance, or an illuminating Book.

34:36 Ease and Limits of Provision

Say: 'My Lord expands or restricts His provision to whomsoever He will, but most of mankind do not know it.'

30:21-22 Duality from Oneness

Another of His signs is that He created spouses from among yourselves for you to live with in tranquillity; He ordained love and kindness between you. There truly are signs in this for those who reflect. Among His signs is the creation of the heavens and earth and the diversity of your languages and colours. In these are signs for mankind.

42:8 One People

Had Allah willed, He would have made them a single community, but He admits into His mercy whomsoever He pleases and the wrongdoers shall have no protector and no ally.

48:1-4 Favours upon the Prophet

We have granted you a conspicuous victory, so that God might show His forgiveness of all your faults, past as well as future, and bestow upon you the full measure of His blessings, and guide you on a straight way, and lend you His mighty aid. It is He Who sent down the tranquillity into the hearts of the believers, that they might add faith to their faith – to God belong the hosts of the heavens and the earth; God is All-Knowing, All-Wise.

48:18 Grace of Serenity

…He knew what was in their hearts, and sent down the spirit of serenity upon them, and rewarded them with news of an imminent victory.

76:31 Mercy and Punishment

For He admits into His mercy whomsoever He will; as for the evildoers, He has prepared for them a painful chastisement.

16:72 Blessing of Offspring

And it is God who has given you spouses from amongst yourselves and through them He has given you children and grandchildren and provided you with good things. How can they believe in falsehood and deny Allah's blessings?

5:54 Love of Allah

O believers, whoso among you shall turn back from his religion, let him know that Allah will bring forth a people whom He loves and who love Him, humble towards the believers but mighty against the unbelievers, who exert themselves in the cause of Allah, and fear no blame from any quarter.

85:14 Forgiveness

…And He is the All-Forgiving, the All-Loving.

55:21 Grace of Acceptance

Which, then, of your Lord's blessings do you both deny?

C. Connectedness & Continuity

2:186 Guidance through Devotion

If My worshippers ask you about Me, I am near. I answer the prayer of him who prays when he prays to Me. So let them obey Me, and believe in Me, perhaps they will be guided aright.

3:29 God, the All-Knowing

Say: 'Whether you conceal what is in your breasts or whether you reveal it, Allah knows it. He knows what is in the heavens and what is on earth. Allah is Powerful over everything.'

3:83 The Universe is in Submission

Can they truly desire anything other than God, when whosoever is in the heavens and on earth submits to Him, willingly or compelled?

7:32 Signs are Meaningful for the Seekers of Knowledge

…We expound the signs for a people who know.

17:85 The Soul

They ask you about the soul, say: 'The soul belongs to the realm of my Lord, and of knowledge you have been granted but little.'

9:51 God's Decrees

Say: 'Nothing will afflict us but what God has decreed for us; He is our Protector; in God let the believers put all their trust.'

8:24 True Life

O believers, respond to God and His Messenger when He calls you to that which grants you life, and know that Allah comes between a man and his heart, and that to Him you shall be gathered.

6:38 Nation of Birds and Other Creatures

There is no creature that crawls on the earth, no bird that flies with its wings, but they are nations like you. We have not neglected any matter in this Book, and then to Allah they shall be gathered.

16:49 All in Prostration

To God prostrate whatever is in the heavens and earth, of the creatures that tread the ground, as do the angels, who display no arrogance.

15:9 Awareness of the Divine

It is We Who have sent down the Remembrance, and We Who shall preserve it.

16:40 God's Will

The only words We say to a thing, when We desire it, is that We say to it 'Be,' and it is.

54:50 Divine Father is in Time and Beyond

When We ordain something, it happens at once, in the blink of an eye.

49:18 Knows and Sees

Allah knows the unseen of the heavens and of the earth; and Allah sees the things you do.

48:23 Divine Consistency

Such being Allah's way which has ever obtained in the past and never will you find any change in Allah's way.

7:180 God's Attributes Desired by Creation

And to God belongs the most beautiful names, therefore call Him by them, and leave alone those who violate the sanctity of His names; they shall be recompensed for what they did.

22:75 Messengers

God chooses Messengers from among the angels and from among mankind; surely Allah is All-Hearing, All-Seeing.

18:27 Constancy of God's Ways

And recite what has been revealed to you of the Book of your Lord, there is none who can alter His words; and you shall not find any refuge besides Him.

25:58 Ever-Living and Knowing

And rely on the Ever-Living Who dies not, and magnify His praise; and Sufficient is He as being aware of the faults of His servants,

24:41 All Glorifies God

Do you not see how all that is in the heavens and earth glorifies God, and the birds with wings outspread? Each has learnt his prayer and his glorification. And God knows full well what they do.

17:44 Everything Glorifies God

The seven heavens and the earth sing His praises, and all who are therein. There is nothing that does not sing His praise, but you do not understand their songs of praise. Surely He is All-Forbearing, All-Forgiving.

31:22 Path of Dedicated Action

Whoever submits his face to God and acts righteously has held fast to a handle most secure. To God belongs the outcome of all affairs.

33:3 Ultimate Reliance

Put your trust in Allah, let Allah suffice as worthy of all trust.

47:7 Dedication to God

O you who believe! If you help Allah, He will help you and will make your foothold firm.

40:55 Patience and Repentance

Therefore, be patient, for the promise of Allah shall come true, and ask forgiveness for your sins, and glorify the praise of your Lord, at evening and dawn.

57:22 Perfect Link between Cause and Effect

No misfortune can happen, either in the earth or in yourselves, that was not set down in writing before We brought it into being, that is easy for Allah.

18:109 God's Commands Are Endless

Say: 'If the sea were ink for the words of my Lord, the sea itself would run dry before the words of my Lord had run dry, even if We provided its like to replenish it.'

57:3-4 God Envelops and Knows All

He is the First and the Last; the Outer and the Inner; He has knowledge of all things. It was He Who created the heavens and earth in six days and then established Himself on the throne. He knows what enters the earth and what comes out of it, what descends from the sky and what ascends to it. He is with you wherever you are, He sees all that you do.

85:20 All-Encompassing

God encompasses them all.

50:16 Closeness of God

And certainly, We created man, and We know what his mind suggests to him, and We are nearer to him than his life-vein.

58:7 Allah Witnesses All

Do you not see that Allah knows everything in the heavens and earth? There is no secret conversation between three people where He is not the fourth, nor between five where He is not the sixth, nor between less or more than that without Him being with them, wherever they may be. On the Day of Resurrection, He will show them what they have done. Allah truly has full knowledge of everything.

20:46 Divine Presence

He said: 'Fear not. I am with you, listening and seeing.'

56:83-85 When the Soul Departs

When the soul reaches the throat. While you gaze on. We are nearer to him than you, but you do not see Us.

62:1 Praise of Allah

Whatever is in the heavens and whatever is in the earth declares the glory of Allah, the King, the Holy, the Mighty, the Wise.

64:8 Allah Witnesses All

So, believe in God, in His Messenger, and in the light We have sent down: God is fully aware of what you do.

65:3 Trust in God is Enough

Whosoever places his trust in God, God shall suffice him. God enforces what He commands. For all things God has set a measure.

76:30 God's Will Prevails Always

And you cannot wish it unless God wishes it. God is All-Knowing, All-Wise.

63:11 Allah Recalls the Soul

Allah does not reprieve a soul when its term has come: Allah is fully aware of what you do.

95:6 Gift of Being at One with God

Except those who believe and do good, so they shall have a reward never to be cut off.

2: Two Zones of Consciousness

The human mind is a faculty that discerns, discriminates and decides what is rational, appropriate and acceptable, and what is to be rejected and deemed irrelevant. This life is the zone of practising to improve the faculty of reason, intellect and rationality, everything we experience is balanced between complementary opposites. As humans we can hold each other accountable and are driven to act in fairness and justice.

We have a natural drive to practice the best of humanity's qualities, such as equanimity, tolerance, acceptance, patience, generosity, and understanding, all of which lead to love as part of the drive to experience unity. The other zone of consciousness is the cosmic source and is not confined or conditioned by space or time, and that is where we assume divinity resides. The maturity and completion of the human purpose in life is to attain a clear and steady mind within a healthy body with a pure heart, so that our humanity is balanced by the boundless lights of divinity and cosmic unity.

Our normal day-to-day consciousness is balanced by the health of all our organs, faculties and well-beingness at all its different levels that constitute the complex human make up, which include physical, chemical, social and other dimensions.

A. Transient Life & Ongoing Life

10:24 Transient Life on Earth

The likeness of this present life is like water We caused to descend from the sky. The plants of the earth, such as men and beasts are wont to eat, grow diverse because of it – until, when earth has assumed its ornament and is decked out in all its finery, and its people think they hold it in their power, Our command descends upon it by night or day, and We turn it into stubble, as though yesterday it had never bloomed. Even so do We make clear the signs for a people who reflect.

18:7-8 Trial of Earthly Attractions

We have appointed all that is on the earth as an adornment for it, and that We may try which of them is fairest in works; and We shall surely make all that is upon it barren dust.

13:26 This Life and Next

God expands and restricts His provision unto whomsoever He will. They rejoice in this present life; and this present life, beside the world to come, is nothing but passing enjoyment.

6:32 Life on Earth and Hereafter

The present life is nothing but play and frivolity, but the final abode is surely better for the pious. Will you not understand?

3:185 Life on Earth and Hereafter

Every self will taste death and you will be paid in full only on the Day of Resurrection. Whoever is kept away from the Fire and admitted to the Garden will have triumphed. And this present life is but the rapture of delusion.

8:28 Earthly Trials

Know that your property and your children are merely a trial, and that with Allah is the greatest reward.

7:51 Punishment in the Hereafter

Those who took their religion for distraction, a mere game, and were deluded by worldly life, today We shall ignore them, just as they have ignored their meeting with this Day and denied our Revelations.

40:39 Life on Earth and Hereafter

My people, this present life is but a passing frivolity, but the hereafter is the Abode of Permanence.

18:45-46 Temporality of Earthly Life

Strike for them a parable of this present life. It is like water We caused to descend from the sky, with which the vegetation of the earth was mingled. But it turned into chaff, scattered by the winds. Allah has power over all things. Property and progeny are the ornament of this present life, but those things that abide, virtuous deeds, are better in reward with your Lord, and better in prospect.

11:15-16 Love of Temporary Life is a Barrier to the Next

Whoso desires the life of this world and its luxuries, to them We pay in full their works; in the world to come there is only the Fire – their deeds there will have failed, and void will be their works.

23:112-115 Earthly Life as Preparation

'How long did you remain on earth?'... 'We remained for a day or a part thereof. Ask those who count.' Do you imagine that We created you in vain? That you will not return to Us?

2:201 Praying for Goodness in this World and the Hereafter

'Our Lord, give us good in this world and in the Hereafter, and protect us from the torment of the fire.'

2:254 Enjoining Generosity

You who believe, give from what We have provided for you, before the Day comes...

3:14 Love of Earthly Pleasures and Wealth

Mankind is tempted with love of delights...

57:20 Illusion and Seduction of Earthly Life

The present life is just a game, a diversion, an attraction, a cause of boasting among you. The life of this world is only an illusory pleasure.

30:7-8 Earthly Leading to Cosmic Life

Their knowledge is only of the appearance of earthly life and as for the hereafter they are distracted. Have they not pondered within themselves? Allah did not create the heavens and earth, and what lies between, except in truth, and for a stated term.

42:36 Short Life on Earth

For all that you have been granted is but a fleeting enjoyment in this present life, but what is with Allah is better and more lasting, for those who believe and place their trust in their Lord.

28:83 Prescription for the Hereafter

There stands the abode of the hereafter, which we have assigned to those who do not seek exaltation on earth, nor corruption. The final outcome belongs to the pious.

3:169 Martyrdom Leads to Lasting Life

Do not think of those who have been killed in Allah's way as dead. They are alive with their Lord, well provided for.

2:94-96 Fear of Death and Desire to Prolong Earthly Life

'If an afterlife with Allah is to be for you alone, to the exclusion of all other people, then you should long for death, if what you say is true!' But they will never wish for it. Allah knows full well who the evildoers are. You will find them clinging to life more eagerly than any other people. Any of them would wish to be given a life of a thousand years.

29:64 Frivolousness of Earthly Life

This present life is nothing but frivolity and amusement. But the Abode of the Hereafter is the real life!

87:16-17 Natural Desire for Earthly Life

Yet, you people prefer the life of this world, though the hereafter is better and more lasting.

B. Balances & Cycles

3:30 Hereafter Reveals All

The Day when every self finds all the good it has done present before it, it will wish all the bad it has done to be far, far away.

3:57 Path

Allah will pay those who believe and do good deeds their reward in full; Allah does not love evildoers.

3:151 Disbelief and Weakness at Heart

We shall cast terror in the hearts of those who disbelieve, for having ascribed partners unto God, for which He has not sent down any authority. And their refuge shall be the fire.

4:111 Misdeeds Against Oneself

He Who commits a misdeed does so against his own self – Allah is All-Knowing and Wise.

6:132 Degrees of States and Stations

All have degrees according to what they have done; Your Lord is not unaware of the things they do.

7:43 Garden of Hereafter

We shall remove all malice from their hearts. They shall say: 'Praise be to Allah Who guided us to this place. The messengers of Our Lord came with the Truth.' And they shall be addressed as follows: 'This is the Garden you have been made to inherit in return for your deeds.'

10:30 All is Revealed in the Hereafter

There and then every soul shall experience what it did in the past, and that which they used to fabricate will forsake them.

10:44 Self Deviation

Allah does not wrong people at all; it is they who wrong themselves.

11:23 Path to Paradise

Those who attain to faith and do righteous deeds and humble themselves before their Lord, they are destined for paradise, and there they shall abide.

21:35 Earthly Trials and Awakening by Death

Every soul shall taste death. We put you to the test, with evil and good, as an ordeal, and to Us you shall return.

23:102-103 Weighty Deeds and Loss of Access to Soul

And as for those whose scales are heavy, they are the prosperous; and as for those whose scale is light, they shall lose their souls...

29:55 Tasting One's Deeds in the Hereafter

He shall say: 'Taste that which you used to commit!'

16:107-108 Attraction of Earthly Life Leads to Darkness and Loss

It is they whom God has put a seal upon their hearts, their hearing and their sight. They are the heedless.

30:41 Decadence and Corruption

Corruption has appeared on land and sea because of what people's hands have earned. He will make them taste part of what they have committed, perhaps they will turn back.

30:44-45 Faith and Disbelief

Whosoever disbelieves, upon him falls his disbelief. Whosoever does a righteous deed, good provision is prepared for their souls, so that He may recompense...

32:14 State of Darkness in Hereafter

So taste it, and since you forgot the encounter of this your Day, We have forgotten you; taste the punishment of eternity for what you have committed.

42:30 Self Affliction

Whatever affliction may visit you is for what your own hands have earned; and He pardons much.

53:39-40 Necessity of Effort

That man will only have what he has worked towards; that his labour will be seen.

78:40 All Revealed on the Day of Reckoning

On the Day when every person will see what their own hands have sent ahead for them, when the disbeliever will say, 'If only I were dust!'

79:34-36 Day of Reckoning

The great predominating calamity comes; on the day that man remembers what he has done, and hell is displayed to whoever can see.

52:16 Reward According to Earthly Actions

You are only being repaid for what you have done.

45:22 Hereafter's Perfect Justice

Allah created the heavens and the earth in truth; every soul may be recompensed for what it has earned; they shall not be wronged.

43:72 Promised Paradise

Such is the Garden bequeathed to you in return for your deeds.

99:7-8 Every Intention or Action Will Be Witnessed

Whoever has done an atom's weight of good shall see it;
Whoever has done an atom's weight of evil shall see it.

C. End of Space & Time

4:87 Resurrection

God! There is no God but He! He shall gather you together upon the Day of Resurrection, of which there is no doubt.

11:4 The Oneness of Origin and Destiny

To God is your return and He holds power over all things.

14:48 New Earth and Heavens

Upon the day the earth shall be changed to other than the earth, and the heavens, and they shall come forth unto God, the One, the Overpowering.

15:85 Creation and Its End

We did not create the heavens and the earth, and all that is between them, save in truth. Surely the Hour is coming; so pardon, with a gracious pardoning.

16:61 Mercy in Delay of Divine Punishment

If Allah were to hold mankind to account for their wrongdoing, He would not leave alive one single creature that treads the earth. He merely defers them until a stated time.

8:47 Universal Collapse

On the day We shall cause the mountains to pass away in motion, and you see the earth void, and bare, We gather them…

21:104 End of the Universe, New Creation

On that Day, We shall roll up the skies as a writer rolls up scrolls. We shall reproduce creation just as We produced it the first time, this is Our binding promise.

22:1 Great Calamity

Be cautiously aware of your Lord, for the quake of the Hour is a mighty thing.

21:1 Illusion of Time

Nearer to mankind their reckoning draws, and yet in heedlessness they turn away.

3:25 Day of Reckoning

How will they fare when We gather them together for a Day of which there is no doubt, when every soul will be paid in full for what it has done, and they will not be wronged.

16:77 The End is Like a Twinkle of the Eye

To God belongs the Unseen in the heavens and in the earth. And the matter of the Hour is as a twinkling of the eye, or nearer.

22:47 Time is Relative

And they demand of you to hasten the chastisement! God will not fail His promise; and surely a day with thy Lord is as a thousand years of your counting.

33:63 End of Universe

People ask you about the Hour. Say: 'Knowledge of it rests with God alone. For all you know, perhaps the Hour has drawn near.'

34:3 Cosmic Collapse

And those who disbelieve say: 'The hour shall not come upon us'. Say: 'Yea! By my Lord, the Knower of the unseen, it shall certainly come upon you; not an atom's weight escapes Him, but that it is in a clear Book.'

52:9-10 Signs of the End of Time

The Day when heaven shall heave in turmoil. And the mountains shall scurry in haste,

56:1-6 The Final Event

When the inevitable event arrives, no one will be able to deny it has come. When the earth is shaken violently, and the mountains are broken down, crumbling, and turn to scattered dust.

77:7-14 Day of Reckoning

What you are promised shall come true. When the stars are erased, and the sky is torn apart. When the mountains are obliterated, and when the Messengers time is set, to what day shall they be delayed? To the Day of Decision. And what will make you comprehend what the Day of Decision is?

44:38-42 Purpose of Creation and Day of Reckoning

We did not create the heavens and earth, and all that between them, in idle play. The Day of Distinction is the term appointed for all of them; a Day when no friend can avail a friend in any way, except such as Allah has shown mercy to; for He is Almighty, Compassionate to each.

29:54 The Wicked Already Face their Destiny of Hell

Hell will encompass all those who deny the truth.

41:54 Denial of the Divine Governance

And yet they are in doubt about the encounter with their Lord, though it is He Who encompasses all things.

53:56-59 Repeated Warnings

This is a warning just like the warnings sent in former times...

78:1-4 The Great News of Truth

Great Tidings. About which they differ? No indeed; they shall soon know!

78:18-20 Day of Reckoning

...you all come forward in multitudes; when the mountains will vanish like a mirage.

81:1-7 Universal Collapse

When the sun is shrouded in darkness. When the stars are dimmed; when the mountains are set in motion; when pregnant camels are abandoned; when wild beasts are herded together; and when the seas are set on fire; when souls are united.

81:10-14 Day of Reckoning

And when the books are spread; when the sky is scraped away; when hell-fire is kindled; when the Garden is drawn near; then each self will know what it has prepared for itself.

101:4-5 Doomsday

On a Day when people will be like scattered moths, and the mountains like tufts of wool.

75:1-25 Resurrection and Full Disclosure of Earthly Conduct

I swear by the Day of Resurrection! No! I swear by the self-accusing soul. Yet man chooses to deny what lies ahead of him. On that Day man will say, 'Where can I escape?' With your Lord alone shall on that day be the place of rest. Man shall on that Day be informed of what he sent before and (what he) put off. Truly, man is a clear witness against himself, even though he offers his excuses. But you love the fleeting, and neglect the hereafter. Upon that Day faces shall be radiant, to their Lord their eyes are lifted; and on that Day there will be the sad and despairing faces, knowing a back-breaker shall befall them.

D. Beyond Space & Time

2:25 The Path to the Garden

Glad tidings to those who have believed and have done good deeds: for them there are gardens. They say: 'This is what we were provided with before' – and they shall be given a likeness of it. In these gardens, they have pure spouses. In them they abide eternally.

2:39 Hell

As for the unbelievers who cry lies to Our signs, those shall be the inhabitants of the fire, therein dwelling forever.

2:82 People of the Garden

While those who believe, and do good deeds will be the inhabitants of the garden, there to remain.

3:15 Gardens of the Hereafter

'Would you like me to tell you of things that are better than earthly joys?' Their Lord will give those who are mindful of Allah gardens graced with flowing streams...

3:162 The Good and the Bad

Is He Who abides by the good pleasure of God like him who turns away, under the censure of God? His refuge shall be hell.

4:57 Path of Victory

Those who believe and do good deeds We shall lead into Gardens beneath which rivers flow, abiding therein forever. In it they shall have pure spouses, and We shall lead them into an overspreading shade.

6:130 Self Will Admit its Waywardness

Were you not visited by messengers from among you, narrating to you My signs and warning you of arriving at a Day like this? They shall say: 'We so witness, against ourselves.' This present life seduced them, and they testified against themselves that they had disbelieved.

7:44 In the Hereafter

The people of the Garden will cry out to the people of the Fire: 'We have found what our Lord promised us to be true. Have you found what your Lord promised you to be true?' and they will answer: 'Yes'. A voice will proclaim from their midst; 'Allah's rejection is on the evildoers.'

9:21 Path to the Garden

Their Lord gives them good tidings of mercy from Him and good pleasure; for them await gardens…

11:108 The Eternal Garden

And as for the happy, they shall be in Paradise, therein dwelling forever, so long as the heavens and earth abide, save as your Lord will, for a gift unceasing.

13:29 Happy Destiny

Of those who believe and do righteous deeds; are destined for happiness and a beautiful return.

13:35 Perfect State in the Garden

Here is a picture of the Garden that those cautiously aware of Allah have been promised: flowing streams and perpetual food and shade. This is the destiny that awaits those who are cautiously aware of God; the disbelievers' destiny is the Fire.

16:111 Day of Reckoning

The day that every soul shall come disputing in its own behalf; and every soul shall be paid in full for what it wrought, and they shall not be wronged.

43:68-70 Entering Paradise

My worshippers, this Day no fear shall fall upon you, nor shall you grieve. Those who believed in Our signs, and had surrendered themselves. 'Enter the Garden, you and your spouses, rejoicing.'

50:34-35 Entering Paradise

'Enter it in peace! This is the Day of Eternity.' Therein they shall have whatever they will; and with Us there is yet more.

55:46 Earthly and Heavenly Gardens

For one who fears to stand before his Lord are two gardens.

57:12-13 Reward and Punishment on the Day of Reckoning

On the Day when you see the believers, both men and women, with their light spreading out ahead of them and to their right, 'The good news for you today is that there are Gardens graced with flowing streams where you will stay: that is truly the supreme triumph!' On the same Day, the hypocrites, both men and women, will say to the believers, 'Wait for us! Let us have some of your light!' They will be told, 'Go back and look for a light.' A wall with a door will be erected between them: inside it lies mercy, outside lies torment.

57:21 Hasten Towards Truth

So race for your Lord's forgiveness and a garden as wide as the heavens and earth, prepared for those who believe in Allah and His messengers; that is Allah's bounty, which He bestows on whoever He pleases. Allah's bounty is infinite.

68:34 Way to Paradise

Surely the God-fearing shall be in Gardens of Bliss with their Lord.

80:33-37 Shocks on the Day of Reckoning

But when the deafening cry comes. That will be a Day when a man flees from his brother, from his mother and his father, from his wife and his children. On that Day will his own state be of sufficient concern.

82:17-19 Absolute Justice on the Day of Judgment

But how can you know what is the Day of Judgment? Indeed, how can you know what is the Day of Judgment? A Day when no soul can do anything to help another. That Day, Judgment belongs solely to God.

3: Creation & Earthly Experiences

Within our earthly womb of space and time there are always beginnings and endings of cycles within cycles that interconnect with everything that exists. We experience a relentless drive to know and to get out of darkness and ignorance towards knowledge and contentment. Knowledges are like ladders that take us up to their source, which is like the centre of the universe, leading to the amazing realisation that the centre is everywhere. This is why the Qur'an declares that "God is everywhere."

With a clearer mind and purer heart, one moves from earthly uncertainty towards the zone from which everything emanates: beyond knowledge and ignorance, certainty and uncertainty. That is from where the light of light radiates throughout the Cosmos. The awakened person knows that all of existence is under perfect governance, always and everywhere.

The divine light is the source, cause, and destination of whatever exists in the heavens and earth. Transitory experiences reflect their timeless source and return to it. In truth, absolute truth permeates the universe but is experienced in diluted and modified ways.

A. Manifestation of Life and Its Diversity

11:7 Earthly Evolvement

And it is He Who created the heavens and the earth in six days, and His Throne was upon the waters, that He might try you, which one of you is best with his duties...

13:2-4 Obvious and Subtle Signs

Allah is He Who raised up the heavens without any pillars that you see. Then He settled firmly on the throne. He made the sun and moon to do His bidding, each running for an appointed time. He governs the world; He makes clear His signs; perhaps you will be convinced of the encounter with your Lord. It is He Who stretched out the earth and set therein firm mountains and rivers, and of every fruit He placed there two kinds...

14:32 Creation

It is Allah who created the heavens and the earth, and sent down water from the clouds, then brought forth fruits to be your sustenance. And He subjected to you the ships... and He subjected to you the rivers.

16:10-11 Water of Life

It is He Who made water descend from the sky, of which some is for you to drink and some for trees from which you pasture. With it He causes vegetation to sprout for your benefit: olives, palms and vines, and all types of fruit. In this there is a sign for a people who reflect.

16:13 Diversity of Creation

Behold what He created for you on earth, diverse in colour; in this there is a sign for people who remember.

16:15-17 Earthly Guidance

He cast upon the earth towering mountains, that it should not shake you violently, and rivers and highways, perhaps you will be guided aright, and waymarks; and by the stars they are guided. Is He Who creates as He Who does not create? Will you not remember?

21:31-32 Sign for Guidance

And We set in the earth firm mountains… and We set in it ravines to serve as ways, that haply they may be guided; and We set up the heaven as a roof well-protected; yet still from Our signs they are turning away.

27:61 Intelligent Differentiations

Is it not He Who made the earth be at rest, and made rivers run through it, and erected mountains therein, and built a barrier between the two seas? Is there to be another god with God? Truly, most of them have no understanding.

32:4 Creation in Stages

It is Allah Who created the heavens and the earth and everything between them in six days . Then He established Himself on the Throne; you have no one but Him to protect you and no one to intercede for you, so why do you not take heed?

20:53 Earth and Water for Life

It is He Who made the earth level for you, and marked out in it highways for you, and made water descend from the sky, through which We caused to come forth pairs of diverse plants.

4:1 Pairs from One Soul

People, be mindful of your Lord, who created you from a single soul, and from it created its mate, and from the pair of them spread countless men and women far and wide; be mindful of God, in whose name you make requests of one another. Beware of severing the ties of kinship: God is always watching over you.

6:98 One Soul/Self

It is He Who brought you forth from one self, a lodging-place, and then a repository. We have made distinct Our signs to a people who understand.

7:189 One Soul in Pairs

It is He Who created you from one self, and made from it a spouse that he might rest in her…

49:13 Creation and Purpose

O mankind, we created you male and female, and made you into nations and tribes that you may come to know one another. The noblest among you in God's sight are the most reverent. God is All-Knowing, All-Aware.

40:64 Human Creation

It is God Who made the earth your place of habitation and the heavens an edifice, He Who gave you form, and made your form attractive, and provided you with pure things. Such is God, your Lord, blessed be God, Lord of the Worlds! He is the Ever-Living,

15:27 Jinn

Whereas the invisible beings We had created, before that, out of the fire of scorching winds.

20:50 Form and Meaning

He said: 'Our Lord is He Who gave each thing its form, and then guided it.'

41:12 Stages and States

Then He ordained seven heavens in two days, and inspired each heaven with its disposition. And We adorned the lowest heaven with lanterns, and for protection. Such was the devising of the Almighty, All-Knowing.

51:47-48 Heavens and Earth

We built the heavens with Our power and made them vast, We spread out the earth, how well We smoothed it out!

65:12 Seven Levels

God is He Who created the seven heavens, and of the earth the like of them; the decree continues to descend among them, that you may know that God has power over all things and that God indeed encompasses all things in His knowledge.

67:2-4 Earthly Life and Death

Who created death and life that He may try you, which of you is best in deeds; and He is the Mighty, the Forgiving, who created the seven heavens one above another; you will see no incongruity in the creation of the Beneficent God; then look again, can you see any disorder? Look again! And again! Your sight will turn back to you, weak and defeated.

54:49 Within Limits

We have created all things in due measure...

B.   Cycles of Life & Death

23:12-16 Process of Human Creation

We created man from the essence of clay. Then We set him a drop, in a receptacle secure. Then We made that drop into a clinging form and We made that form into a lump of flesh, and We made that lump into bones, and We clothed those bones with flesh, and later We made him grow into another creation. Glory be to God, the best of creators! Then after that you shall surely die, then on the Day of Resurrection you shall surely be raised.

6:95 Cycles of Life and Death

It is God Who splits open the seed and the pits. He causes the living to issue from the dead, and the dead to issue from the living. Behold the works of God! How can you deny?

2:28 Resurrection

How can you disbelieve in Allah when you were once dead, and He granted you life? He shall cause you to die, then He shall resurrect you, then to Him you shall return.

6:60 Facing One's Deeds

It is He Who causes you to die by night, and knows what you earn by day. Then He sends you forth therein, until a stated term is fulfilled. Then to Him is your return. Then He shall inform you of your deeds.

30:19 Life and Death

He brings forth the living from the dead and the dead from the living; He revives the earth after its death, and thus will you too be brought forth.

22:66 Earthly Life, Death and Eternal Life

It is He Who gave you life, will cause you to die, then will give you life again, but man is ungrateful.

39:42 Experiencing Life and Death

God takes the selves of the dead and the selves of the living while they sleep – He keeps hold of those whose death He has ordained and sends the others back until their appointed time – there truly are signs in this for those who reflect.

31:28 One Soul is the Origin of All Humans

Your creation and resurrection are only as if you were a single self. Allah is All-Hearing, All-Seeing.

41:39 Life on Dead Earth

And of His signs is that you see the earth humble; then when We send down water upon it, it quivers, and swells. Surely, He Who gives it life is He Who gives life to the dead; surely, He is powerful over everything.

43:11 Life, Death and Resurrection

And Who sent down water from the sky in due measure; and We revived thereby a land that was dead; even so you shall be brought forth.

20:55 From Earth, to It and then Resurrection

From it We created you, to it We shall return you, and from it We shall once more resurrect you.

15:21 In Measures from Source

There is not a thing, but its treasuries are with Us, and We do not send it down but in a known measure.

71:17-18 Birth, Death and Resurrection

And God caused you to grow out of the earth, then He will return you into it and then bring you out again.

85:13 Earthly Life and Hereafter

It is He Who brings people to life, and will restore them to life again.

2:260 Living from Dead

When Abraham said: 'Lord, show me how you revive the dead.' He said: 'Have you not believed?' Abraham said: 'Yes, but so that my heart can be at peace.' He said: 'Take four birds, cut them in pieces and place each piece upon a separate mountain. Then call them and they shall come flying to you. Know that God is Almighty, All-Wise.'

6:133 Cycle of Creation

Your Lord is Self-Sufficient, Possessor of Mercy. If He wishes, He can make you disappear and appoint whomever He wishes as successors after you, just as He created you from the progeny of other nations.

14:19 Purpose of Creation is to Connect Directly with the Creator

Do you not see that Allah created the heavens and the earth in truth? If He will, He can remove you away and bring a new creation.

C. Orbits & Opposites

10:5-6 Wonders of Creation

It is He Who made the sun a radiance, and the moon a light, and determined for it phases that you might know the number of the years and the reckoning. God did not create that except by truth, distinguishing the signs for a people who know. In the succession of night and day, and in what Allah created in the heavens and earth, there truly are signs for those who are cautiously aware.

31:29 In Succession

Do you not see how God makes the night enter into the day and makes the day enter into the night, He has made the sun and moon subservient, each of them running to a stated term, and that Allah is aware of what you do?

39:5 Successions

He created the heavens and the earth in truth, wrapping night about the day, and wrapping the day about the night; and He made the sun and the moon subservient, each of them running to a stated term. Is not He the Almighty, the All-Forgiving?

28:73 Dualities of Action and Rest

It is a mercy from Him that He created for you the night and the day, in which you may find rest or seek His bounty; perhaps you will give thanks.

25:53 Two Waters

It is He Who made the two seas flow, one sweet and fresh and the other salty and bitter, and put an insurmountable barrier between them.

35:12 Two Zones

The two seas are not alike: this one is fresh and sweet water, tasty to drink, that one salty and bitter. From both you eat flesh that is soft, and you extract gems to wear. Therein you can see ships ploughing through the waves, that you may seek of His bounty – so that you give thanks.

55:19-20 Dualities Appear as Separate

He brought the two seas together, yet there is a barrier between them which they do not transgress.

55:5-8 Cosmic Mercy and Compassion

The sun and the moon follow their appointed courses; and the stars and the trees prostrate themselves. He has raised up the sky. He has set the balance. Do not transgress the Balance.

78:6-8 Dualities

Did We not make the earth smooth, and the mountains as pegs? And We created you in pairs…

51:49 Pairs from One

And We created pairs of all things so that you might reflect.

14:33 Gifts of Nature

He subjected to you the sun and moon constant upon their courses, and He subjected to you the night and day.

17:12 Signs of the Night

We made night and day to be two signs, and We erase the sign of night and cause the sign of day to appear to the eyes, so that you may seek bounty from your Lord, and learn the computation of years and accounts. All things have We clarified most clearly.

21:30 Universal Expansion and Splitting

Do the unbelievers not realize that the heavens and earth were sewn together, but We ripped them apart, and from water created every living thing? Will they not believe?

D. Darkness & Lights

14:1 Darkness to Light

This is a Book We have sent down to you that you may bring forth mankind from the darkness to the light by the leave of their Lord, to the path of the Almighty, the All-Praiseworthy.

14:5 Darkness to Light

We sent Moses with Our signs: Bring your people from the darkness into the light. Remind them of the Days of God, there truly are signs in this for everyone patient, thankful.

6:1 Creation of Dualities

Praise be to God Who created the heavens and the earth, and appointed the darkness and light; And yet those who disbelieve set up equals to their Lord!

6:122 Illumined or in Darkness

Is then He Who was dead and whom We thereupon gave life, and for whom We set up a light whereby he might see his way among men, like one in darkness deep, out of which he cannot emerge? Thus it is made to seem good all their own doings to those who disbelieve.

4:174 Divine Light and Proof

People, convincing proof has come to you from your Lord and We have sent a clear light down to you.

2:257 Darkness to Light and the Reverse

God is the ally of those who believe: He brings them out of the depths of darkness and into the light. As for the disbelievers, their allies are false gods who take them from the light into the depths of darkness, they are the inhabitants of the Fire, and there they will remain.

2:14 Dishonesty and Hypocrisy

When they meet the believers, they say: 'We believe,' but when they are alone with their evil ones, they say: 'We're really with you, we were only mocking.'

2:74 Hardness of Heart

Then your hearts became hardened thereafter and are like stones, or even yet harder; for there are stones from which rivers come gushing, and others split, so that water issues from them, and others crash down in awe before Allah. And Allah is not heedless of the things you do.

2:171 Dead and the Living

The likeness of those who disbelieve is like one who bellows to a creature that cannot give ear to anything save 'Come!' or 'Go!' Deaf. Dumb. Blind. They do not understand.

2:18 Deadened

Deaf. Dumb. Blind. They do not return.

13:16 Relative and Absolute Truth

Say: 'Who is the Lord of the heavens and earth?' Say: 'Allah.' Say: 'So have you taken to yourselves instead of Him, protectors who have no power over what benefit or harm may come to themselves?' Say: 'Is the blind man the equal of one who sees? Or is darkness the equal of light? Or have they fashioned partners to Allah who created something like His creation, and so creation became a matter that perplexed them?' Say: 'Allah is the Creator of all things; He is One, Overpowering.'

4:168-169 Way to Hell

Allah will not forgive those who have disbelieved and do evil, nor will He guide them to any path, but the road that leads to hell, therein to abide eternally and this is indeed easy for Allah.

7:179 No Insight

We have consigned to hell many jinn and humans. They have hearts but do not understand, eyes but do not see, ears but do not hear. They are like cattle – indeed more astray! Those, they are the mindless.

7:186 Total Loss

Whosoever God causes to be lost, there will be no guide for him and will be left to stumble in their arrogance.

7:198 Inner Blindness

If you call them to right guidance they do not hear. You see them looking at you but they do not see.

11:24 Some Blind and Deaf Yet Others Not

The likeness of the two groups is like the blind and deaf, and the one who sees and hears: are they equal in likeness? Will you not remember?

39:22 Belief and Heart

Consider where he whose breast God opens for submission, such that he follows a light from his Lord? Woe unto those whose hearts are hardened for abandoning the remembrance of God! These are in flagrant error.

45:20 Insights

This is a means of insight for mankind, and a guidance and grace unto people who are endowed with inner certainty.

43:36 Forgetting the Merciful

Whoso turns away from the Remembrance of the All-Merciful, to him We assign a satan for comrade...

57:9 Darkness to Light

It is He Who has sent down clear revelations to His Servant, so that He may bring you from the depths of darkness into light; Allah is truly kind and merciful to you.

12:96 Light of Insight

But when the bearer of good news arrived and threw the tunic on his face, he recovered his sight and said: 'Did I not tell you that I know from God what you do not know?'

17:45-46 Barriers to Spiritual Light

And when you recite the Qur'an, We place between you and those who do not believe in the hereafter a hidden barrier; Upon their hearts We draped veils, such as they do not understand, and in their ears heaviness. Should you happen to mention in the Qur'an that your Lord is One, they turn tail, and withdraw in aversion.

22:46 The Path

What, have they not journeyed in the land so that they have hearts to understand or ears to hear? It is not the eyes that are blind, but blind are the hearts that turn away.

17:72 Earthly Life a Prelude to the Hereafter

Those who are blind in this world, in the hereafter will be even more blind and more astray from the path.

7:101 Sealed Hearts

These are the towns whose stories we have recounted unto you.; their Messengers came to them with the clear signs, but they were not the ones to believe in that they had cried lies before; so Allah seals the hearts of the unbelievers.

18:57 No Guidance

And who does greater evil than He Who, being reminded of the signs of his Lord, turns away from them and forgets what his hands have forwarded? Surely, We have laid veils on their hearts, such as they do not understand it, and in their ears heaviness; and though you call them to the guidance, they will not be guided ever.

20:124-126 Loss

Whoso turns away from remembrance of Me shall live a life of hardship, and We shall herd him on the Day of Resurrection, blind. He shall say: 'My Lord, why do you herd me blind when before I could see?' He said, 'Even so it is. Our signs came unto you, and you forgot them; and so today you are forgotten.'

7:27 Story of Adam

O Children of Adam, do not let Satan seduce you as he drove out your two parents from the Garden. He stripped them of their garments to show them their shame... We have assigned the devils as masters of those who do not believe.

47:23 Blind and Deaf

These are the ones God has rejected, making their ears deaf and their eyes blind.

83:13-15 Denial Leads to Darkness

When Our revelations are recited to him, he says, 'Ancient fables!' No indeed! Their hearts are encrusted with what they have done. No indeed! On that Day they will be screened off from their Lord...

61:8 God's Light

They aim to extinguish God's light with their utterances: but God has willed to spread His light in all its fullness, however hateful this may be to all who deny...

35:19-22 Differentiations

Unequal are the blind and those who see; Nor is darkness and the light, or shade and heat; unequal are the living and the dead. God hears whom He pleases, but you cannot make them hear, those who are in their graves.

E.   Signs, Metaphors & Parables

2:242 Signs

God makes plain His signs to you; perhaps you will understand.

2:106 Arc of Ascent

For every sign We abrogate or cause to be forgotten, We bring one better or similar. Do you not already know that Allah has power over all things?

16:36 Guidance through Messengers

To every nation We sent a messenger: 'Worship God and shun false deities.' Some of them God guided aright; some deserved to be led astray. So journey in the land and observe how the fate of the deniers turned out.

12:111 Reflections

In their narratives is a lesson to those possessed with intellect. This is no tale being spun but a confirmation of what came before it, a clear explication of all things, and a guidance and a mercy to the faithful.

14:24-26 True Metaphor

Do you not see how Allah draws a parable: A good word is like a good tree; its roots are firm and its branches reach to the sky. It brings forth its nourishment at every turn, by its Lord's leave. And Allah draws parables for mankind; perhaps they will remember. But an evil word is like a rotten tree, uprooted from the surface of the earth, with no power to endure.

17:1 Prophet's Night Journey

Glory be to Him Who carried His servant by night from the Sacred Mosque to the Furthest Mosque, whose precincts We have blessed, to show him of Our wonders! He it is Who is All-Hearing, All-Seeing!

27:93 Wonders of Creation

Praise be to Allah! He shall show you His wonders, and you shall recognize them; nor is your Lord heedless of what you do.

40:13 Repentance and Remembrance

It is He Who shows you His signs and sends down to you out of heaven provision; yet none remembers but He Who repents.

36:80 Creation

Who has made for you out of the green tree fire and behold, you kindle from it.

30:21-22 Duality from Oneness

Another of His signs is that He created spouses from among yourselves for you to live with in tranquillity: He ordained love and kindness between you. There truly are signs in this for those who reflect. Among His signs is the creation of the heavens and the earth, and the diversity of your languages and colours. In these are signs for mankind.

39:27 Reflect upon Meaning

In this Qur'an, We have struck for mankind every sort of parable; perhaps they will remember.

45:3-4 Signs for the Faithful

In the heavens and earth are signs for those who believe. As also in your creation, and in the creatures He dispersed; are signs for a people of firm faith.

41:53 Signs on the Horizons and Within

We shall show them Our signs on all horizons and in their very selves, until it becomes obvious to them that it is the Truth. Does it not suffice that your Lord is a witness of all things?

30:52-53 Potential and Willingness to Understand Necessary

You cannot make the dead hear, nor make the deaf hear the call, if they turn and walk away. You will not guide the blind out of their error neither will you make any to hear except those who believe in Our signs, and surrender.

30:58 Qur'an Guidance

We have struck for the people in this Qur'an every manner of parable…

27:12 Purified Intention

Put your hand inside your cloak and it will come out white, without fault. These are among the nine signs that you will show Pharaoh and his people; they have really gone too far.

26:61-68 Story of Moses's Crossing

And, when the two hosts saw each other, the companions of Moses said, 'We are overtaken!' he said: 'No, truly my Lord is with me and will guide me.' We inspired Moses: 'Strike the sea with your staff, and it split open, each side like a towering mountain.' Then We brought the others near, and We delivered Moses and those with him all together; then We drowned the others. Surely in that is a sign, yet most of them are not believers. It is your Lord Who is Almighty, Compassionate to each.

10:92 Saving the Body of Pharaoh

So today We shall save your body so that you may be a sign to those after you. Surely many men are heedless of Our signs.

7:203 Guidance for Believers

…Here are visible proofs from your Lord, a Guidance and a mercy to a people of faith.

25:45 Constant Light and Changing Shadows

Have you not seen how your Lord has lengthened the shadow? Had He willed, He could have stood it still. The sun We made as a pointer to it.

26:121 Most are at a Loss

In this was a sign, but most of them were not believers.

12:105 Ignored Signs

And there are many signs in the heavens and the earth that they pass by and give no heed to.

35:27-28 Diverse Creation

Do you not see that God sends down water from the cloud, then we bring forth fruits of various colours; and in the mountains, are streaks white and red, of various hues and others intensely black; And of humans, beasts of burden and cattle of diverse colours? From among his worshippers, only the learned fear God. God is Almighty, All-Forgiving.

30:16 Earthly and Cosmic Life

But as for those who disbelieved, and rejected Our signs and the encounter of the Hereafter, they shall be brought over to chastisement.

6:104 Sight and Insight

Insight has come to you from your Lord. So whoever sees clearly, it is to the benefit of his own soul. And whoever is blind, it is to its detriment and I am not a keeper over you.

56:71-74 The Origin is Ingrained Within the Soul

Have you ever considered the fire which you kindle? Is it you who produced the tree of it or We? We have made it to be a reminder – and too, a comfort to hungry travellers. So, glorify the name of your Lord, the Supreme.

54:17 Qur'an

We have made it easy to learn lessons from the Qur'an: will anyone take heed?

4: Humanity & Conditioned Consciousness

The principle gift of life is awareness and consciousness. Sentiency begins with the birth of a baby and the mind begins to build a network of neuron circuits that enables the child to connect stimulus with response. The growing child will begin to have preferences as to what it likes and dislikes, which are functions of nature and nurture that lead to the development of a personality. A teenager experiences a complex sense of self or ego which is constantly being modified within a dynamic field of individual and communal affiliations.

As we interact with other living creatures through empathy, sympathy, and the fulfilment of other needs, conditioned consciousness evolves and leads to higher consciousness, towards the magical realization of unity in perpetuity. That is the eternal zone of Cosmic Oneness. Personal as well communal social habits, religions and cultural norms help to bring about stability as well as movement towards completion of awakening to pure consciousness.

A. The Human Journey & The Arc of Consciousness

2:30-31 Creation of Adam

And when your Lord said to the angels: 'I am appointing a viceroy on earth,' they said: 'Will You put someone there who will cause discord and bloodshed, when we celebrate Your praise and proclaim Your holiness?' but He said: 'I know things you do not.' And He taught Adam all the names, then presented them to the angels; then He said: 'Tell me the names of those if you are truthful.'

7:11-12 Adam and Angels Prostration

And certainly, We created you, then We fashioned you, then We said to the angels: 'Prostrate to Adam.' So they did prostrate, except Iblis; he was not of those who prostrated. He said: 'What prevented you from prostrating when I commanded you?' He said: 'I am better than he. You created me of fire but him You created of clay.'

15:32-40 Shaytan

He said: 'O Iblis! What is thy reason for not being among those who have prostrated themselves? …surely you are accursed. Upon you shall fall a curse until the Day of Judgement.' …Iblis said: 'I shall make the earth attractive to them, and lure them all away, except for your sincere servants among them.'

7:19 Adam in Paradise

O Adam! Dwell you and your wife in the garden; so eat from where you desire, but do not go near this tree, for then you will be of the wrongdoers.

7:23-25 Adam's Descent to Earth

They said: 'Our Lord, we wronged ourselves. If You do not forgive us and be merciful towards us, we shall surely be lost.' He said: 'Descend, enemies one to another! On earth you shall have a dwelling place and livelihood for a while.' He said: 'In it you shall live; in it you shall die; from it you shall be brought forth.'

20:115-123 Temptation of Adam

We entrusted Our revelation to Adam in days gone by, but he forgot, and We found in him no steadfastness. We said, 'Adam, surely this Iblis is an enemy to you and your wife. So do not let him expel you both from the Garden, so that you should be in misery.' And Adam disobeyed his Lord, and went astray. Then his Lord… pardoned him, and guided him. He said: 'Descend from it, both of you, an enemy one to another. When guidance comes to you from Me, whoso follows My guidance shall neither stray nor be wretched.'

16:78 To Express Gratitude

It is Allah who brought you out of your mothers' wombs knowing nothing, and gave you hearing and sight and hearts, so that you might be thankful.

76:1-3 Human Rise

Was there not a time when man was nothing to speak of? We created man from a drop of mingled fluid to put him to the test; We gave him hearing and sight; We guided him upon the way, be he grateful or ungrateful.

67:23 Senses and Heart

Say: It is He Who brought you into being, Who provided you with hearing, sight and hearts, but little thanks do you give.

40:67 Stages of Human Growth

It is He Who created you from dust, then from a drop of fluid, then from a tiny, clinging form, then He brought you forth as infants, then He allowed you to reach maturity, then He let you grow old – though some of you die sooner and reach your appointed term so that you may reflect.

36:68 Rise and Falls

And whomsoever We cause to live long, We reduce (him) to an abject state in constitution; do they not then understand?

95:4-5 High and Low States of Human

We indeed created Man in the fairest stature, then reduce him to the lowest of the low.

46:15 Gratitude, Life on Earth, Bringing Up

…he says: 'My Lord, inspire me to be thankful for Your blessings, which You bestowed on me and my parents, and that I act in virtue, pleasing to You. Grant me a virtuous progeny; truly I turn in repentance to You, and truly I am among those who submit.'

30:54 Human Strength and Weakness Inseparable

God is He that created you of weakness, then He appointed after weakness strength, then after strength He appointed weakness and grey hairs; He creates what He will, and He is the All-Knowing, the All-Powerful.

17:70 Spread of Adam's Children

We honoured the progeny of Adam and carried them on land and sea. We provisioned them with delicacies and preferred them far above many whom We had created.

33:72 Heavenly Trust

We offered the Trust to the heavens, the earth and the mountains, but they declined to carry it and were afraid of it, but man carried it and he has ever been unjust, intemperate.

51:56 Purpose of Life

I created jinn and mankind only to worship Me.

2:35-38 Human's Fall and Rise

And We said, 'Adam, dwell with your wife in the garden… but do not go near this tree'. Satan made them slip, and removed them from the state they were in. We said, 'Go down, you are each other's enemy. On earth you will have a place to stay and livelihood for a time.' Then Adam received words from his Lord and pardoned him, He is the Ever-Ready to pardon; He is Compassionate to each. We said: 'Go down from it, all of you. And when My guidance comes to you, whoever follows My guidance, no fear shall fall upon them, nor shall they grieve.

B.   Human Nature & Desires

4:173 Doers of Good and the Arrogant

To those who believe and do good works He will give due rewards and more of His bounty; to those who are disdainful and arrogant He will give an agonizing torment, and they will find no one besides Allah to protect or help them.

34:34 Wealth and Indolence

We sent no warner to any town without its men of luxury saying: 'We disown what you have been sent with…'

63:9 Dunya Attractions

Believers, do not let your wealth and your children distract you from remembering God: those who do so will be the ones who lose.

2:87 Egotistic

…So how is it that, whenever a messenger brings you something you do not like, you become arrogant, calling some impostors and killing others?

100:6-8 Lower Nature of Man

Most surely man is ungrateful to his Lord. And most surely, he is a witness of that. He is truly excessive in his love of wealth.

9:55 Distraction of Earthly Wealth

So do not be impressed by their wealth or their progeny; God only desires to punish them thereby in this present life, and their souls shall expire while still unbelievers.

6:116 Most are at a Loss

If you obey most of those on earth they will lead you astray from the path of God; they follow only surmise, merely conjecturing.

17:11 Human Folly

Mankind may seek evil, instead of praying for good; mankind is ever hasty.

18:54 Wisdom of the Qur'an

In this Qur'an, We have elucidated to mankind every sort of parable, and man is, of all beings, the most argumentative.

9:97 Uncouth Desert Dwellers

The Arabs of the desert are severe in unbelief and hypocrisy, and more disposed not to know the limits of what God has revealed to His Messenger; and Allah is All-Knowing, All-Wise.

16:22 Arrogance and Disbelief

Your God is the One God. As for those who deny the life to come, their hearts refuse to admit the truth and they are arrogant.

64:14-15 Worldly Attractions, Earthly Distractions

O you who believe! Surely from among your wives and your children there is an enemy to you; therefore, beware of them; and if you pardon and forbear and forgive, then surely God is Forgiving, Merciful. Your wealth and your children are only a test for you. There is great reward with God.

2:206 Arrogance Leads to Hell

When he is told, 'Beware of Allah,' his arrogance leads him to sin. Hell is enough for him: a dreadful resting place.

47:38 Spending in the Way of Allah

Here you are, called upon to expend your wealth in the cause of God. Some of you begrudge this, and whoso begrudges it is merely begrudging himself! God is All-Sufficient, and it is you who are poor. And if you turn away, He will substitute another community for you, and they shall not be like you.

89:17-20 Love of Wealth

Nay! you do not honour the orphan, nor do you urge one another to feed the poor, and you devour the inheritance greedily, and you love wealth with exceeding love.

79:37-39 Love of Dunya

Whoever then has exceeded all bounds, and prefers the life of this world, surely Hell shall be the refuge.

2:78 Ignorance

And some common folk not knowing the Book, but only fancies and mere conjectures.

62:11 Dunya Attraction

And when they see some commerce or diversion, they rush toward it and leave you (Prophet) standing there. Say: 'God's gift is better than any entertainment or trade: God is the best provider.'

10:22 Forgetfulness

It is He Who causes you to journey on land and sea, until when you are aboard ships... a raging storm arrives, and the waves surround them on all sides... it is then that they call upon God, in all sincerity of faith, 'If You deliver us from this ordeal, we shall truly be thankful.'

4:116 Darkness of Dualities

God does not forgive that anything be associated with Him, but forgives what is less than this to whomsoever He pleases. Whoever associates anything with God has indeed strayed far.

4:17 Repentance

But God accepts repentance from those who do evil out of ignorance and soon afterward repent: these are the ones Allah will forgive, He is All-Knowing, All-Wise.

74:16-23 Worst Conduct

No! He has been stubbornly hostile to Our revelation, (and so) I shall constrain him to endure a painful uphill climb! He reflected and assessed, curse him how he assessed! and curse him again how he assessed. Then he looked, then he frowned and scowled, and turned away and behaved arrogantly

79:46 Day of Reckoning

On the Day they see it, it will seem they lingered in this life an evening at most, or its morning.

21:37 Nature of Creation

Mankind was created hasty; and I shall show you My wonders, so do not be in haste.

70:6-7 Presence of Truth

They see it far, but We see it near.

C. Affliction & Ease

7:94-96 Faith, Piety and Transgression

Never did We send a prophet to a city but We seized its inhabitants with hardship and injury; perhaps they might repent in humility. Then We substituted good for evil until they grew prosperous and said: 'Our ancestors too were touched by both hardship and ease.' But suddenly We seize them, unawares! Had the people of the cities believed and grown pious We would have opened to them the blessings of heaven and earth. But they lied, so We seized them in recompense for what they earned.

2:155-156 Trials and Shortage

We shall be testing you with some fear and famine, with loss of wealth, lives and crops: but give glad tidings to the patient, those who say, when afflicted with a calamity, 'We belong to Allah and to Him we shall return.'

3:186 Earthly Distractions

You shall be put to a hard test as regards your wealth and your selves, and you shall hear much harm from those who were given the Book before you, and from the idolaters. But if you bear with patience and fear Allah, this will be a course of action upright and resolute.

4:28 Humans are Weak

Allah wishes to lighten your burden; man was created weak.

11:9 Quick to Despair

And if We let a man taste mercy from Us, and then We wrest it from him, he is desperate, ungrateful.

6:165 Test and Trial on Earth

It is He Who made you inheritors of the earth, and elevated some of you above others in degree to test you in what He bestowed upon you. Your Lord is swift in punishment; your Lord is All-Forgiving, Compassionate to each.

22:11 Weak Belief

Among people is one who worships Allah, on condition. If good befalls him, he grows content with it. But if an ordeal befalls him, he turns his face about, losing this world and the next. This is the most manifest loss.

23:75 Virtue of Suffering

If We show them mercy and draw away the hardship they suffer, they would persist in their outrage, groping in blindness.

30:36 God's Mercy Interrupted by Mischief

And when We let men taste mercy, they rejoice in it; but if some evil befalls them for that their own hands have forwarded, behold, they despair.

29:2-3 Earthly Life as Preparation for Hereafter

Do people imagine they will be left to say 'We believe', and are not put to the test? We put to the test those who came before them, that God may make it known who were sincere and who were lying.

61:10-12 Path to Bliss

O you who have attained to faith! Shall I point out to you a bargain that will save you from grievous suffering in this world and in the life to come? You are to believe in God and His Apostle, and to strive hard in God's cause with your possessions and your lives… He will forgive you your sins, and in the life to come will admit you into gardens through which running waters flow, and into goodly mansions in those gardens of perpetual bliss: that will be the triumph supreme!

35:34 In Grace

And they shall say, 'Praise belongs to Allah who has removed all sorrow from us. Surely our Lord is All-Forgiving, All-Thankful…'

92:4-10 Paths of Ease and Hardship

As for him who gives and is God-fearing, who testifies to goodness; We shall smooth his way towards ease. And as for him who is miserly… and disbelieves in God's reward, We shall smooth his way towards hardship.

94:5-6 Ease and Difficulty Together

So truly where there is hardship there is also ease; truly where there is hardship there is also ease…

90:4 Struggle is Natural

We have created man for toil and trial.

70:19-21 Man's Nature

Man was truly created anxious; whenever misfortune touches him, he is filled with self-pity; and whenever good fortune comes to him, he selfishly withholds it from others.

28:10 Secure Heart

But the heart of Moses' mother became empty, and she would have disclosed it, had We not strengthened her heart, that she might be among the believers.

64:11 Guidance

Misfortunes can only happen with God's permission – He will guide the heart of anyone who believes in Him: God knows all things.

85:11 Path of Success

Those who believe, and do righteous deeds, for them await gardens underneath which rivers flow; that is the great triumph.

29:10 Human Mischief, not God's Punishment

There are people who say: 'We believe in God.' If one meets with harm in the cause of God, he considers the harm done by other people as God's punishment.

8:25 Suffering for Many

And beware an ordeal which will afflict not merely the wrongdoers among you, and know that God is severe in His punishment.

67:10-12 To Hear, Understand and Fear

And they shall say: 'Could we but hear or understand, we would not be among the dwellers of Hell.' They will confess their sins. Away with the inhabitants of the blazing fire! But there is forgiveness and a great reward for those who fear their Lord though they cannot see Him.

63:6 Not Forgivable

It is all the same if you seek or do not seek forgiveness for them, for God shall not forgive them. God guides not the transgressors.

13:34 Double Suffering

Torment awaits them in this present life but the torment of the hereafter is more terrible. From Allah they can expect no one to shield them.

3:126 The Good News

God did not intend this revelation except as glad tidings to you and so that your hearts may be reassured by it. Victory comes solely from God, the Almighty, the Wise.

19:33 Direct Connection of Jesus to the Source

Peace be upon me the day I was born, the day I die, and the day I am resurrected, alive!

D. Self Deception & Truth

2:8-10 Faith is Not Only by Pronouncement of Tongue

And there are some people who say: 'We believe in God and the last day'; and they are not at all believers. They desire to deceive God and those who believe, and they deceive only themselves and they are not aware. There is a disease in their hearts, so God added to their disease and they shall have a painful chastisement because they used to lie.

2:42 Truth

And do not confound the truth with falsehood, or hide the truth when you know it.

4:111-113 Misdeeds against Oneself

He Who commits a misdeed does so against his own self – God is All-Knowing and Wise. And whoever commits an offense or a sin, and then casts it upon one who is innocent, bears the burden of calumny and a manifest sin. Were it not for Allah's grace upon you and His mercy, a group among them had endeavoured to lead you astray – but it is themselves they lead astray. Nor will they harm you in any way, for God has revealed to you the Book and the Wisdom and taught you that which you did not know. The bounty of God upon you has been ever great.

29:66 Truth Will Be Revealed to All

…They will come to know.

3:85 Path of Islam

Whoso desires a religion other than Submission, this shall not be accepted from him, and in the afterlife he will be among the losers.

3:90 Ultimate Loss

Those who disbelieved after their belief and increased further in disbelief: their repentance shall not be accepted. These are the truly wayward.

4:38 Wrongdoers

Those who spend their wealth to show off, who do not believe in Allah or the Last Day. Whoever has Satan for companion, what a wretched companion he has!

4:142 Self-Deceivers

The hypocrites seek to deceive God but it is He Who deceives them. If they rise to prayer, they rise reluctantly, dissembling before people. They remember God but little.

6:5 Denial of Truth

They denied the Truth when it came to them; but there shall come to them a true account of that which they used to mock.

7:99 God's Ways Beyond Human Mind

Do they really feel secure from the cunning (subtle plan) of Allah? None can feel secure from the cunning of Allah save those who are lost.

12:106 Earthly Duality Confuses

And the most part of them believe not in Allah, but they associate other gods with Him.

8:21-22 Deaf and Dumb

And be not as those who say, 'We hear,' and they hear not. Verily, the vilest of all creatures in the sight of God are those deaf and dumb ones who do not understand.

9:82 Future of Evil Ones

They shall laugh a little and weep a lot, in recompense for what they have earned.

9:67 Evilness of Hypocrisy

Hypocrites, male and female, are all alike: they command what is forbidden and forbid what is virtuous, and clench tight their hands. They have forgotten God and so He has forgotten them. The hypocrites are the dissolute.

10:36 Confusion

Most of them merely follow conjecture, but conjecture can never substitute for the truth. God is All-Knowing as to what they do.

18:50 Story of Adam

When We told the angels, 'Prostrate yourselves before Adam,' they all prostrated themselves, save Iblis: he was one of the jinn, but then he turned away from his Lord's command. Will you, then, take him and his seed for masters instead of Me, although they are your foe? How vile an exchange for the evildoers.

14:18 Ignorance is Loss

The deeds of those who reject their Lord are like ashes that the wind blows furiously on a stormy day: they have no power over anything they have gained. This is to stray far away.

16:20-21 Most are in Darkness

And those they call upon, apart from God, created nothing, but are themselves created; dead, not alive, and are not aware when they shall be raised.

18:103-105 Failure and Loss

Say: 'Shall We tell you who will be the greatest losers in their works? Those whose striving goes astray in the present life, while they think that they are working good deeds.' Those are they that disbelieve in the signs of their Lord and the encounter with Him; their works have failed, and on the Day of Resurrection We shall not assign to them any weight.

29:41 Seeking Security

The likeness of those who took to themselves patrons instead of God is like the spider that builds a house for itself. But surely the most fragile of houses is the spider's house, if only they knew.

39:29 Clear or Confused Direction

Allah strikes a parable: a man shared by partners at loggerheads, and a man belonging wholly to another man – can the two be equal in likeness? Allah be praised! In truth, most of them are ignorant.

13:42 Allah's Will Prevails

Those before them also practiced their cunning, but to God belongs all cunning. He knows what each self earns, and the unbelievers shall surely know to whom belongs the destiny of the Abode.

17:10 Disbelief in Hereafter

But as for those who do not believe in the hereafter We have prepared a torment most painful.

27:50-52 The Master Plotter

And they worked their plot, and We worked Our plot, of which they were unaware. Behold the outcome of their plotting! We destroyed them and their people, outright. There stand their habitations, desolate because of their wickedness. In this is a sign to a people who understand.

36:19 Accountability

…'Your destiny, good or evil is upon you'…

39:49 Tests

When man suffers some affliction, he cries out to Us, but when We favour him with Our blessing, he says, 'All this has been given to me because of my knowledge', it is only a test, though most of them do not know it.

47:1 Nullified Effort

Those who disbelieve and turn away from God's way, We shall nullify their efforts.

39:63 God Governs All

To Him belong the reins of the heavens and earth. But those who disbelieved God's revelations, they are the losers.

6:11 Explore and Reflect

Say: 'Travel the earth and see what was the destiny of liars.'

3:137 God's Laws Apply at All Times

Many generations have passed away before your time, so journey in the land and observe to what end the deniers have come!

6:123 Leaders Often Mislead

And so We have placed chief criminals in every city to perpetrate their schemes there – but they scheme only against themselves, without realizing it.

7:4 Without Progress to the Higher, there is Regression and Destruction

How many towns We destroyed! Our wrath came upon it as they slumbered at night or reposed by day.

15:4-5 Destiny

We did not destroy any town without it having run its set course. No community can bring its time forward, nor delay it.

26:208 Warnings Before Destruction

We never destroyed a city, but that it had its warners.

16:112 Affliction Due to Ingratitude

God strikes a simile: a town, once secure and content, its livelihood coming to it in plenty from all directions, which then denied the blessings of God. He made it taste the utmost of hunger and fear because of what they did.

17:16 Most Disasters are Man Made

If We desire to destroy a town, We command the affluent in it, yet they indulge in transgressions, so Our just decree comes to pass upon it, and We destroy it utterly.

18:58-59 Actions Balanced by Response

Your Lord, All-Forgiving, Abounding in Mercy; were He to hold them to account for what they earned, He would hasten their punishment. Indeed, an appointed time is set for them, and they shall find no escape from it. We destroyed these cities when they perpetuated injustices, and set an appointed time for their destruction.

28:59 The Wicked Will Self Destroy

Your Lord would not have destroyed these towns unless He had first sent a messenger to their capital city, reciting Our revelations. Nor would We have destroyed these towns unless their inhabitants were wicked.

27:34 Corruption of Rulers

She said: 'When kings enter a city they corrupt it, and reduce its most honourable people to abject misery. This is how they act.'

40:21 Explore and Reflect

Have they not journeyed in the land and observed the end of those who preceded them? They were greater than them in might, and left behind more landmarks on earth. And yet God seized them for their sins, and they had none to shield them from God.

35:39 Disbelief

It is He Who appointed you stewards in the earth. So whoever disbelieves, his unbelief shall be charged against him; their unbelief increases the disbelievers only in haste of Allah's sight; their unbelief increases the disbelievers only in loss.

35:44 Evidence of Temporariness of Superiority

Have they not travelled in the land and seen how those before them met their end, although they were superior to them in strength? God is not to be frustrated by anything in the heavens or on the earth. He is All-Knowing, All-Powerful.

53:50-52 End of Ancient Nations

And He Who destroyed ancient 'Ad, and Thamud, leaving no trace of them, and before them the people of Noah who were even more unjust and insolent…

9:80 No Guidance for the Rejecters of Truth

It makes no difference whether you ask forgiveness for them or not: Allah will not forgive them even if you ask seventy times, because they reject Allah and His Messenger. Allah does not guide the rebellious people.

3:154 God is the Cause of All but Humans are Responsible for Actions

After sorrow, He caused calm to descend upon you, a sleep that overtook some of you. Another group, caring only for themselves, entertained false thoughts about Allah… 'Everything to do with this affair is in Allah's hands.' They conceal in their hearts things they will not reveal to you… those who were destined to be killed would still have gone out to meet their deaths. Allah did this to test everything within you and to prove what is in your hearts. Allah knows your innermost thoughts very well.

47:5-12 Guidance

He will guide them and improve their condition, and admit them into the Garden He made known to them. O you who believe! If you help Allah, He will help you and will make you steadfast. But as for the unbelievers, ill chance shall befall them! He will send their works astray… God shall surely admit those who believe and do righteous deeds into gardens underneath which rivers flow.

68:44 Downward Distraction

So (Prophet) leave those who reject this revelation to Me: We shall lead them on, step by step, in ways beyond their knowledge.

E. Religions, Cultures & Habits

3:19 Submission to the Way of God

The true religion with God is submission. Those who were given the Book were not at variance except after the knowledge came to them, being insolent one to another. And whoso disbelieves in God's signs, God is swift at the reckoning.

3:64 Inter Faith

Say: 'People of the Book, let us rally around a discourse common to us and you: that we worship none but God, that we associate nothing with Him, that we do not take each other as lords apart from God.' If they turn away, say: 'Bear witness that we submit.'

4:26 Path

God wishes to make clear to you and to guide you concerning the laws of those who came before you, and to pardon you. God is All-Knowing, All-Wise.

10:19 One Mankind

All people were originally one single community, but later they differed. If it had not been for a word from your Lord, the preordained judgement would already have been passed between them regarding their differences.

5:57 Seriousness of the Path

O believers, do not take for allies those who took your religion as a subject of mockery and entertainment among those granted the Book before you, or among the unbelievers. Be cautiously aware of God if you truly believe.

15:10-11 Affliction of Prophets

And We have sent others before you to various groups of ancient peoples, but never did a messenger come to them except that they mocked him.

6:91 God is Beyond Measure, Reflectivity Regarding Scriptures

Nor have they honoured Allah as He ought to be honoured when they say that Allah did not send down anything to a human being. Say: 'Who was it who sent down the Book that Moses brought, a light and guidance to mankind, which you have committed to scrolls, some of which you show and much of which you hide? And then you were taught what you did not know, neither you nor your fathers.' Say: 'It is Allah,' then leave them to indulge in their frivolity.

6:4 Habit of Distraction

Not a sign of their Lord comes to them, but they turn away from it.

3:67 Islam of Abraham

Abraham was neither a Jew nor a Christian. He was upright and devoted to God, never an idolater.

26:69-92 Story of Abraham

And recite to them the story of Abraham, when he said to his father and people: 'What is it that you worship?' They said: 'We worship idols and minister diligently to them.' He said, 'Do they hear you when you call, or benefit you or do you harm?' They said: 'Rather, we found our forefathers so doing.' He said: 'Do you realize what you have been worshipping, you and your ancient forefathers? Surely, they are enemies to me, but not the Lord of the worlds; He it was Who created me, and He it is Who guides me; and Himself gives me to eat and drink, When I am sick He cures me; Who makes me to die, then gives me life, and Who, I hope, will forgive me my faults on the Day of Recompense.'
'My Lord, give me Judgment, and join me with the righteous, and appoint me a tongue of truthfulness among the others. And make me of the heirs of the garden of bliss, and forgive my father, for he is one of those astray. Do not disgrace me the Day they are resurrected, a Day when neither wealth nor progeny shall be of any worth, except one who approaches Allah with a pure heart.' The Garden shall be drawn near to the pious, and hell shall be revealed to the fiendish. And it shall be said to them: 'Where are those that you used to worship?'

44:22-28 Confession, Warning, Distraction and Loss

So he prayed to his Lord: 'These are a wicked people.' (and God said) 'Set out at night with My worshippers, but you will surely be pursued, and leave the sea behind you calm and still, for they are a troop that will surely be drowned. They left how many gardens and fountains, sown fields, and how noble a station, and what prosperity they had rejoiced in! Even so; and We bequeathed them to another people.'

10:84-86 Saving Moses

Moses said, 'O my people, if you believe in God, in Him put your trust, if you have surrendered.' They said, 'In God we have put our trust. Our Lord, make us not a temptation to the people of the evildoers, and save us, by Thy grace, from people who deny the truth!'

22:67 Traditional Habits

For every nation We established a ritual that they follow, so do not allow them to dispute this matter with you. And call to your Lord, for you are upon a path of right guidance.

30:32 Pleased with what is Familiar

Those who have split apart their religion and turned into sects, each sect happy with what they have.

6:159 Divisions within Religions

Those who have made divisions in their religion and become sects, you have nothing to do with them; their affair is with God, then He will tell them what they have been doing.

5:104 Blindly Following Ancestors

If it is said to them: 'Come to what God has sent down and to the Messenger,' they retort: 'Sufficient for us is what we find our ancestors have followed.' What! Even if their ancestors knew nothing, and lived without guidance?

31:21 Adherence to Old Habits

And if it is said to them: 'Follow what God has sent down,' they answer: 'Rather we shall follow what we find our forefathers had followed.' Even if Satan is calling them to the torment of a raging Fire?

43:23-24 Habits of Past

Likewise, We sent no warner before you to any city but its men of luxury would say: 'We found our forefathers set on this course, and are following in their footsteps.' Say: 'What! though I bring you a better guidance than you found your fathers following?' They say; 'We disbelieve in that you were sent with.'

11:117-118 Safety in Goodness; One Humanity

And yet your Lord would not have destroyed cities unjustly if their inhabitants had been virtuous. Had your Lord willed, He would have created mankind a single nation. But they continue to differ.

37:71 Forefather's Way

Thus, indeed, most of the people of old went astray before them.

43:6-7 Prophets

How many prophets we sent among the ancients, but not a prophet came to them, without their mocking at him.

42:14 Differences

They differed after Knowledge had come to them, out of mutual envy. Were it not for a prior Word from your Lord which set a stated term, judgment would have been passed on them. And those bequeathed the Book after them are in perplexing doubt about it.

49:14 Faith and Belief

The Bedouins say: 'We believe.' Say: "You do not believe. Instead you may say: 'We surrender,' but faith has not entered your hearts. If you obey God and His Messenger, God will not diminish your works in any way." God is All-Forgiving, Compassionate to each.

4:49-50 Purification

Have you not considered those who call themselves pure? It is God, rather, who purifies whomever He pleases, and they shall not be wronged one fleck.

5: Wholesome Living

Most intelligent human beings are driven by hope and good expectations to be content and happy. Up until a few generations ago most human communities were often guided by the feeling of responsibility to others and what was considered ethical, moral and noble conduct. The main drive was kindness, goodness to others and a willingness to sacrifice personal desires and benefits for the good of others and for the principle of lasting goodness and truth.

The family, tribe and community were still held in high respect and honour until the latter part of the 20th century. Then a major shift and drift from conventional and traditional ethics and morality began to take place globally, and personal welfare and contentment became the ultimate goal of most people. Many people consider this shift as unhealthy and selfish. In truth, selflessness and selfishness are seamlessly connected. Selfishness will lead to decadence and destruction whereas the ultimate joy in life is in losing one's self or ego in order to experience the unbounded soul.

Wholesome living is to accept the ways of the world without succumbing to the mainstream pursuits of acquisition, accumulation and the false security in purely material issues. Wholesome living is to accept humanity with its needs and limitations and yet be in constant reference to the perpetual lights of Divinity. Frequent resonance between mind and heart are necessary conditions to the state of joyful well-beingness. In essence we are heavenly and only earthly as part of a process of preparation for the next state of the hereafter, beyond the restrictions of space and time.

A. Glad Tidings & Warnings

2:2-7 Conduct of the Believers and Those in Denial

That is the Book, wherein there is no doubt, a guidance to the cautiously aware. Who trust in the Unseen, and uphold the prayer, and expend of that We have provided them; and who faithfully trust in that which has been revealed to you and that which was revealed before you and they are certain of the hereafter. Those are truly guided by their Lord, and those who will prosper. As for the deniers, it is all the same if you warn or do not warn them: they will not believe. God has set a seal upon their hearts and upon their hearing and there is a covering over their eyes, and there awaits them a great torment.

2:218 Human Struggle in the Way of Truth is Necessary

Those who believed, and those who emigrated and exerted themselves in the path of Allah, they can indeed expect the mercy of Allah. Allah is All-Forgiving, Compassionate to each.

7:178 The Guided and the Lost

Whoever God guides is truly guided; whoever He leads astray, they are truly the losers.

3:178 Earthly Respite for the Unbelievers

And let not the unbelievers suppose that the indulgence We grant them is better for them; We grant them indulgence only that they may increase in wrongdoing; and there awaits them a humbling chastisement.

7:155 Divine Plot Prevails on Earth

A trial from You; through it You lead astray whomsoever You will, and guide aright whomsoever You will. You are our Protector. Forgive us, the Most-Forgiving.

6:125 Relief Due to Surrender and Constriction for the Lost Ones

When God wishes to guide someone, He expands their breast for submission. When He wishes to lead them astray, He closes and constricts their breast...

8:70 Goodness Only Increases

If God knows of any good in your hearts, He will give you more than what was taken from you, and will forgive you...

10:4 Awakening to Truth for All

To Him you shall all return: a true promise that He began creation and will then restore it, to reward those who believed and performed good deeds in fairness. For those who disbelieved, there awaits a drink of boiling water and painful torment because of their denial.

17:15 Guidance and Loss, for and against Oneself

Whosoever is guided, is only guided to his own gain, and whosoever goes astray, it is only to his own loss; none shall bear the burden of another.

17:82-84 Healing

We send down the Qur'an as healing and mercy to those who believe; as for those who disbelieve, it only increases their loss… Everyone acts according to his state; but your Lord knows who is best guided in the path.

8:10 Contented Due to Revelation

As good news, and so that your heartsmight be calmed thereby.

27:2-6 Glad Tidings and Warning

Guidance and glad tidings to the faithful, who perform the prayer, hand out alms and are certain of the hereafter… those who do not believe in the hereafter, We have made their deeds appear attractive in their sight, so they stumble aimlessly… who shall be the greatest losers in the hereafter.

32:19-22 Believers in the Garden and the Unbelievers in Affliction

Those who believed and did righteous deeds, to them belong the Gardens of Refuge as an abode and reward for their works. The dissolute, however, shall have the Fire as their refuge. We shall make them taste the lesser torment rather than the greater, perhaps they might return.

26:90-92 The Garden and Hell Already Close at Hand

The Garden shall be drawn near to the pious, and hell shall be revealed to the fiendish.

34:28 For All Mankind, Everywhere and All Times

We have not sent you but to all of mankind as a bearer of good news, and warner; but most men do not know it.

36:11 Warnings Help Whoever Desires Truth

Warn him who follows the Remembrance... to him give glad tidings of forgiveness and a noble wage.

47:14 Believer vs Non-Believer

So, is He Who is certain of his Lord like one to whom his misdeeds are made to appear attractive, and who pursue their whims?

45:15 Self Awakening or Loss

Whoever does righteousness, it is to his own gain, and whoever does evil, it is to his own loss; then to your Lord you shall be returned.

78:4-5 Truth Will Be Revealed to All

Certainly, they shall know and indeed for sure they shall know.

B. Self-Soul Dynamics

2:138 God's Colours and Attributes

The hue of God is upon us! And what better hue than God's? It is Him we worship.

4:79 God is the Source of Good whereas Evil is Self-Inflicted

Whatever good befalls you comes from God; whatever evil befalls you comes from your own selves. We have sent you to mankind as a messenger.

8:53 Loss of Grace due to Wrong Attitude

God would never change His favour that He conferred on a people until they changed what was within themselves.

10:108 Save Yourself from the Lower Self

Say: 'O mankind, the Truth has come to you from your Lord. Whoso embraces guidance, embraces guidance for his own soul's good; whoso goes astray, leads his own self astray. Nor am I your guardian.'

12:53 Divine Soul Saves from Evil Self

...The self ever urges to evil, except when my Lord shows mercy...

103:1-3 The Self Loses and the Soul is Triumphant

Surely man is in loss, all save those who believe, who do righteous deeds, who enjoin truth… who enjoin patience.

7:172 Every Human Soul Knows the Truth

Your Lord took away from Adam's children the seeds from their loins, and made them witness upon themselves, 'Am I not your Lord?' They answered: 'Yes, we witness' – lest you should claim on the Day of Resurrection: 'We were unaware of this.'

6:164 Every Self Earns Its Destiny

…Every self earns only to its own account, none shall bear the burden of another…

6:12 Loss of Soul and Failure

Say: 'To whom belongs what is in the heavens and earth?' Say: 'To Allah. He has pledged upon Himself mercy in order that He may gather you together on the Day of Resurrection, of which there is no doubt.' But those who have lost their selves, they do not believe.

13:11 Focus Upon Soul is the Path

…God does not change what is in a people, until they change what is in themselves…

7:42 To Do One's Utmost is the Path

And those who believe and perform good deeds, We do not charge a self except with what it can bear, these are the people of the Garden, therein dwelling forever.

2:286 Prayers and Pleading for Goodness

God does not burden any self with more than it can bear: each gains whatever good it has done, and suffers its bad…

2:216 What is Liked and Disliked Not Always Conducive for Illumination

…you may hate something and it is good for you… you may love something and it is harmful to you. God knows.

60:7 Attraction and Repulsion for Friends and Enemies

God will create affection between you and those among them with whom you were in enmity.

29:6-7 Earthly Life as Preparation for Hereafter

Whoso exerts himself does so for his own benefit. And Allah has no need of the worlds and those who believe, and do righteous deeds.

32:13 Personal Effort Necessary for Guidance

We could indeed have imposed Our guidance upon every human being.

91:7-10 Grooming of Self

By the self, and the proportion and order given to it; and inspired it to know its own rebellion and piety! He will indeed be successful who purifies it. And he will indeed fail who corrupts it.

33:4 One Direction

Allah did not place two hearts inside a man's chest.

50:21 Inner Drive and Witness

And every soul shall come, with it a driver and a witness.

59:19-20 Awareness Necessary for the Garden

Do not be like those who forget God, so God causes them to forget their own higher selves: they are the rebellious ones. There is no comparison between the inhabitants of the Fire and the inhabitants of Paradise – and the inhabitants of Paradise are the successful ones.

23:62-63 All According to Divine Decree

We do not charge a soul except with what it can bear. With Us is a Book that utters the Truth, and they shall not be wronged… but their hearts are in perplexity as to this, and they have deeds besides that which they are doing.

70:40-42 Common Desire for the Best and Distraction towards the Worst

So I swear by the Lord of the easts' and wests' that We are able to replace them with what is better than them; and none outstrips Us.

C. Responsibility & Accountability

2:284 Allah Sees and Knows All

Whatever is in the heavens and in the earth belongs to Allah and, whether you reveal or conceal your thoughts, Allah will call you to account for them.

16:93 One Humanity but Different Nations

Had God willed, He would have made you a single nation.

2:272 Guidance is Only from Allah and Goodness Benefits One's Own Self

It is not for you to guide them; it is Allah who guides whoever He will. Whatever charity you give benefits your own self, provided you do it for the sake of God, whatever you give will be repaid to you in full, and you will not be wronged.

16:89 Guidance of the Book

And the day We shall raise up from every nation a witness against them from amongst them, and We shall bring you as a witness against those. And We have sent down on you the Book making clear everything, as a guidance and a mercy, and as good tidings to those who surrender.

17:71 Judgment in the Hereafter

…We shall call all men with their record…

17:13 Thoughts and Action Will Be Fully Witnessed

And for every man we have made his actions cling to his neck; and We shall bring forth for him, on the Day of Resurrection, a book he shall find spread wide open.

41:20-22 Every Cell Tells the Story

…their own ears, eyes and skins shall testify as to what they used to do… 'Allah gave us speech, He Who gave speech to all things.' It was He Who created you the first time, and to Him you have been returned… you imagined that God does not know most of what you do.

39:70 Total Accountability

Every soul shall be paid in full for what it has wrought; and He knows very well what they do.

54:52-53 All Actions are Recorded

Everything they do is noted in their records: every action, great or small, is recorded.

48:17 Clear Judgement

No blame upon the blind, the lame or the sick…

59:18 Necessity for Greater Awareness

Be mindful of God, and let every self consider carefully what it sends ahead for tomorrow; be mindful of God, for God is well aware of everything you do.

74:37-39 Dignified Conduct for All

Every soul shall be held in pledge for what it has earned.

57:28 God's Inner Guiding Light

O believers, be cautiously aware of God and believe in His messenger and He will double your share of His compassion, and shine His light upon the path you tread, and forgive you. God is All-Forgiving, Compassionate to each.

82:5 Day of Reckoning

Each soul will know what it has done and what it has left undone.

75:13 Everything Revealed Upon Resurrection

Man shall on that day be informed of what he did before and what he put off.

78:29 Full Reckoning Upon Resurrection

But We have placed on record every single thing of what they did.

35:45 Mercy of Delayed Accountability

Had God taken people to task for what they earned, He would not have left a crawling creature on the face of the earth. Instead, He postpones them to a stated term.

80:11-12 Qur'an as Reminder to Remember

No indeed; it is a Reminder, and so whoever is willing may remember Him.

17:14 The Self Will Know and Admit

Read your Book. Let your own self suffice you now as accountant.

D. Appropriate Conduct

2:152 Remembrance and Gratitude

So remember Me; I will remember you. Be thankful to Me, and never ungrateful.

2:195 Goodness Wards Off Destruction

Spend in Allah's cause: do not contribute to your destruction with your own hands, but do good, for God loves those who do good.

2:225 What is in the Heart Matters Most

God will not take you to task for oaths which you may have uttered without thought, but will take you to task for what your hearts have conceived...

2:263 Goodness Without Harm

A kind word and forgiveness is better than a charitable deed followed by hurt: God is Self-Sufficient, Forbearing.

3:114 The Righteous

They believe in Allah and the Last Day; they command virtue and forbid vice; they hasten to do good deeds. These are among the righteous.

4:110 God is Ever-Forgiving

Yet anyone who does evil or wrongs himself and then asks God for forgiveness will find Him most Forgiving, Compassionate to each.

4:135 Total Honesty

...uphold justice and bear witness to God, even if it is against yourselves, your parents, or your close relatives.

4:58 Trust and Justice

...return trusts to their owners and, when you judge between people, to judge with fairness.

8:27 Trustworthiness

...do not knowingly betray your trusts.

63:10 Charity

Give out of what We have provided for you, before death comes to one of you.

93:9-11 Generosity, Kindness and Gratitude

As for the orphan, do not oppress him. And as for him who asks, do not repel him, and talk about the blessings of your Lord.

2:275-276 Usury Forbidden

Those who take usury will rise up on the Day of Resurrection like someone tormented by Satan's touch. That is because they say, 'Trade and usury are the same,' but God has allowed trade and forbidden usury.

65:7 Charity According to Means

God does not burden any soul with more than He has given it – after hardship, God will bring ease.

17:29 Appropriate Conduct

Do not withhold from giving, nor overextend in sharing that which you have, or else you will end up worthy of blame, regretful.

14:31 The Path towards Hereafter

Tell My servants who have believed to keep up the prayer and give, secretly and in public, out of what We have provided them, before a Day comes when there will be no trading nor befriending.

15:88 Modesty

Do not long for what we have given pairs of them to enjoy; and do not be sorry for them; and lower your wing to the believers.

34:37 Ease and Limits of Provision

It is not your wealth nor your children that shall bring you in nearness to Us, except for him who believes, and does righteousness; theirs is a manifold reward for what they did, and they shall be secure in the lofty chambers.

9:105 Striving Will Be Acknowledged

Say: 'Strive, and God shall see your striving, as also His Messenger and the believers. You shall be returned to the Knower of the Invisible and the Visible, and He will inform you of what you used to do.'

11:10-11 Arrogance and Patience

...He becomes exultant and boastful, except those who bear with patience and perform good deeds...

17:23 Patience and Kindness to Parents

Your Lord decrees that you worship none but Him, and graciousness to parents. If they attain old age with you, either or both, say not to them: 'Phew!' and do not scold them but speak to them words of kindness.

7:204 Courtesy to Qur'an

When the Qur'an is recited, listen to it and remain silent; so that perhaps you will be shown mercy.

58:12 Reverence and Courtesy

O believers, if you wish to converse in privacy with the Messenger, offer a gift in charity before your intimate conversation, for this would be better for you and purer. If unable to do so, Allah is All-Forgiving, Compassionate to each.

28:77 Earthly Life is Transit to Hereafter

But seek amidst that which God has given you, the Last Abode, and do not forget your portion of the present world; and do good, as God has been good to thee. And do not corrupt the earth; surely God does not love the workers of corruption.

31:16-19 Correct Behaviour

'O my son, if it should be but the weight of one grain of mustard-seed, and though it be in a rock, or in the heavens, or in the earth, God shall bring it forth; surely God is All-Subtle, All-Aware. Keep up the prayer, my son; command what is right; forbid what is wrong; bear anything that happens to you steadfastly: these are the most honourable of traits. Do not turn your cheek away from people in contempt, and do not walk exultantly upon the earth, God loves not every swaggering snob. Let your walk be modest and keep your voice low: the ugliest of sounds is the braying of an ass.'

47:33 Obedience

O believers, obey God, and obey the Messenger, and do not make your own works vain.

38:26 Justice and Accountability

'David, behold, We have appointed you a viceroy in the earth; therefore judge between men justly, and do not follow caprice, lest it lead you astray from the way of God. Surely those who go astray from the way of God for them there awaits a terrible chastisement, for having forgotten the Day of Reckoning.'

70:33-34 Charity and Honesty

Those who abide by their trusts and their pact, who give honest testimony.

5:90 Abhorrence of Alcohol and Gambling

O believers, intoxicants and gambling, idols and divining arrows are an abhorrence, the work of Satan. So keep away from them, that you may prosper.

51:15-19 Generosity of the Pious

Truly the reverent are amidst Gardens and Springs, taking whatsoever their Lord has given them; they were virtuous before that. Sleeping only little at night and in the mornings, they would ask for forgiveness. In their wealth beggars and the deprived had a rightful share.

73:8-10 Celebrate the Divine Attributes

So celebrate the name of your Lord and devote yourself wholeheartedly to Him. Lord of the East and West – there is no God but He! Accept Him as Patron. Patiently endure what they say, ignore them politely.

51:20-22 Signs of Truth All Around

On earth there are signs for those with sure faith. And in yourselves too, do you not see? In the heaven is your sustenance and all that you are promised.

57:23 Be Present and Content

…grieve not for what you have missed, nor be exultant at what He has given you; and God does not love any arrogant boaster.

94:7-8 Higher Consciousness Emerges from Lower Consciousness

When your earthly work is done, turn to devotion, and turn to your Lord for everything.

61:2-3 Do What You Say or Promise

Why do you say what you do not do? It is most hateful to God that you should say that which you do not do.

E.   People of the Middle Way

2:177 The Right Path

The truly good are those who believe in God and the Last Day, in the angels, the Book, and the prophets; who give away some of their wealth, however much they cherish it… who are steadfast in misfortune, adversity, and times of danger. These are the ones who are true, and it is they who are aware.

2:110 Good Deeds are for Yourself

Whatever good you put forward for yourselves, you will find it with God, He sees everything you do.

11:85 Fairness and Balance

'My people, give full share in the measure and balance, acting justly. Do not cheat people of their goods and do not act wickedly on earth, corrupting it.'

4:13 Boundaries Needed for Victory

These are the bounds set by God. God will admit those who obey Him and His Messenger to Gardens graced with flowing streams, and there they will stay – that is the supreme triumph!

2:285 Messengers are the Same in Their Messages

The Messenger believes in what was revealed to him from his Lord, as do the believers. All believe in God, His angels, His Book and His messengers.

9:71 The Righteous

The believers, male and female, are friends of one another. They command to virtue and forbid vice. They perform the prayers and pay the alms, and they obey God and His Messenger. To these, God shall show them mercy. God is Almighty, All-Wise.

4:100 Migrating in the Way of God

Who emigrates in the cause of Allah shall find on earth many places of emigration and abundance. Whoso leaves his home as an emigrant to Allah and His Messenger and is overtaken by death, his reward falls upon Allah, and Allah is All-Forgiving, Compassionate to each.

3:132 Mercy Flows from the One

Obey God and the Messenger, so that you might be shown mercy.

18:30 Straight Path

Those who believed and performed good deeds...

20:81-82 Warning of Exceeding the Limits

Do not exceed the limits, or My wrath shall fall upon you. He upon whom My wrath falls will sink to the depths… and yet I am All-Forgiving towards him who repents, and believes, and does good deeds, and then is guided aright.

9:112 The Path

The repentant, the worshippers, the thankful, the fasting, those who kneel and prostrate themselves, the bidders to good and forbidders of evil, the respecters of the bounds of God – give glad tidings to the believers!

9:18 On the Path of the Guided

Those who believe in God and the Last Day, and perform the prayer, and pay the alms, and fear none but God alone; it may be that those will be among the guided.

2:179 Punishment and Justice

The prospect of retribution saves lives, O you who are possessed of intellect — perhaps you will be cautiously aware.

49:10-12 Conduct towards Others

All believers are brethren. Hence, make peace between your two brethren... be graced with His mercy... Refrain from backbiting one another... avoid undue suspicion, for some suspicions are sinful. Do not spy on one another or speak ill behind one another's back... And fear God, for God is All-Pardoning, Compassionate to each.

19:96 Guidance

But those who believed and did good deeds, the All-Merciful shall show them love.

60:13 Who to Befriend

O believers, do not ally yourselves with people upon whom God's wrath has fallen. They have abandoned all hope of the Hereafter, just as the unbelievers have abandoned all hope of resurrection for those who dwell in graves.

23:1-5 Path of Victory

Prosperous are the believers; they who in prayer are humble, who abstain from idle chatter, who constantly fulfil the obligation of alms giving, who guard their chastity.

6: The Web of Cosmic Oneness

The basic human drive is to connect with what we consider is important or desirable and to maintain and continue that connection. The natural drive toward higher knowledge is a gift of nature driving us toward higher consciousness. During the past several thousand years in many communities on earth we had periods of a high quality life and well-beingness at physical and emotional levels, as well as in terms of the spiritual qualities and higher consciousness. We are driven towards greater consciousness and to what gives us hope and optimism regarding contentment and happiness. Human life is a process of learning and awakening to a state of full illumination. The mother is the first teacher, leading to teachers who can help us with skills and discernible knowledges, as well as teachers of inner knowledge to help awaken to the light within our own soul.

Every human life is work in progress from basic consciousness that helps to survive, grow and develop towards the higher reaches of spiritual awakening to the ever-prevalent truth – the eternal, cosmic light of lights. Our desire for connection, love and power are indicators that awakening to infinitude is the completion of one's duty and purpose in life. It is then that one realises the complete and perfect interconnectedness of everything that exists in the universe. This state is referred to as God's control and governance of all.

A. Revelation

2:2 Qur'an as the Book of Cosmic Unveiling

That is the Book, wherein is no doubt, a guidance to the cautiously aware.

3:3-4 Scriptures

He has sent down upon thee the Book with the truth, confirming what was before it, and He sent down the Torah and the Gospel before: a guidance to mankind.

3:7 Clarity of Scriptures and Doubters

It is He Who sent down the Book upon you. In it are verses precise in meaning: these are the very heart of the Book. Others are allegorical. Those in whose heart is waywardness pursue what is ambiguous therein, seeking discord and seeking to unravel its interpretation…

7:2-3 The Book of Reality and Truth

A Book sent down to you, so let there be no distress in your breast due to it. You are to warn with it, and it is a Remembrance to the believers.

7:145 Prophetic Revelation for Moses

…So, grasp them firmly and command your people…

13:1 Signs and Indications for Believers

Those are the signs of the Book; and that which has been sent down to you from your Lord is the truth, but most people do not believe.

20:2-3 Awakening for Sincere Seekers

We did not bring down the Qur'an upon you to make you suffer, but only as a remembrance to all who stand in awe.

17:88 Unique Miracle of Qur'an

Say: 'Were humans and jinn to band together to produce a semblance of this Qur'an, they could not do so, even if they backed one another up.'

28:85 Qur'an Guides to Source

He Who ordained the Qur'an upon you shall return you back to origin. Say: 'My Lord knows best who brings guidance and who is in manifest error.'

42:52-53 Revelation as Guidance to All Who Qualify

There was a time when you did not know what the Book was, nor faith, but We brought it forth as a light by which We guide whomever We will of Our servants. And you are assuredly guiding to a straight path, the path of God, to Whom belongs all that is in the heavens and earth. In truth, all matters shall revert to God.

29:49 Pure Heart Reads the Truth

…It contains revelations most clear in the hearts of those granted knowledge…

39:23 Guidance for Spiritual Beings

God has sent down the most perfect discourse: a Book consistent and recapitulating. At the mention of it, the skins of those who fear their Lord shudder, but then their skins and hearts grow soft at the remembrance of God. Such is God's guidance: through it God guides whomever He pleases. And whom God leads astray, no guide has he.

59:21 Power of Truth is Immense

If We had sent this Qur'an down upon a mountain, you would have seen it humbled and split apart in awe of God. We offer people such illustrations so that they may reflect.

73:5 Truth Will Dispel All Else

Behold, We shall cast upon you a weighty word.

65:11 Gardens of the Hereafter

God will admit those who believe in Him and do righteous deeds into Gardens graced with flowing streams, where they will remain forever – He has made good provision for them.

B. Prophetic Being

2:136 All Prophets Equal in Their Spiritual State

Say: 'We believe in Allah, and in what was revealed to us, in what was revealed to Abraham, to Ishmael, to Isaac and Jacob and the Tribes, in what was revealed to Moses and Jesus, in what was revealed to prophets by their Lord. We make no distinction between any of them, and to Him we surrender.'

2:253 Prophets Differ in Their Effect Upon People

We favoured some of these messengers above others. God spoke to some; others He raised in rank; We gave Jesus, son of Mary, Our clear signs and strengthened him with the holy spirit...

6:48 Good News and Warning

We send messengers only as heralds of glad tidings and warners. Whoso believes and does good deeds, no fear shall fall upon them, nor shall they grieve.

3:31 Love of Truth

Say: 'If you love God, follow me and God will return your love, and forgive you your misdeeds. God is All-Forgiving, Compassionate to each.'

3:164 Messenger from the People to Guide them

Allah is gracious to the believers in sending them a Messenger from among their own, to recite His signs to them, to make them grow in purity, and to teach them the book and wisdom – before that they were clearly astray.

9:33 Triumph of Truth

He it is Who sent His Messenger with Guidance and the religion of truth, that He may exalt it above all religions.

9:128-129 The Way of the Prophet

A messenger from among your own, aggrieved by the hardship you suffer, concerned for you, tender and compassionate towards the believers.

6:50 Sights, Insights and Revelation

Say: 'I do not tell you that I possess the treasures of God, nor do I know the Unseen. Nor do I tell you I am an angel. I merely follow what is revealed to me.' Say: 'Is the blind man the equal of one who sees? Will you not reflect?'

14:4 Guidance and Clear Communication

And We have sent no Messenger save with the language of his people, that he might make all clear to them; then God leads astray whomsoever He will, and He guides whomsoever He will…

18:110 Revelations are Flashes of Truth from Higher Consciousness

Say: 'I am but a human being like you, to whom revelation is sent…'

11:36-37 Story of Noah

And it was revealed to Noah, saying, 'None of your people shall believe… Build the Ark where We can see you…'

7:144 Prophetic Consciousness

He said: 'Moses, I have chosen you above all men for My messages and My utterances; so take what I have given you, and be of the thankful.'

79:16-20 Prophetic Mission

When his Lord called to him in the holy valley, Tuwa: "Go to Pharaoh, for he has exceeded all bounds, and ask him, 'Do you want to purify yourself? So I can guide you to your Lord, and you come to fear Him?'" So he showed him the great sign.

19:12 Commitment to the Book

'O John! Take firm hold of the Book.' And We granted him sound judgment...

19:16 Story of Mary

And mention in the Book Mary, when she withdrew from her people to an eastern place.

19:25 Story of Mary

So shake towards you the trunk of the palm and it will drop down on you dates, soft and ripe.

25:56 Glad Tidings and Warnings Come Together

And We sent you, only as a herald of glad tidings and a warner.

48:8 Gladness and Warnings Together

We have sent you as a witness, a bearer of glad tidings and a warner.

19:76 Guidance

God shall increase those who were guided in guidance…

42:51 Divine Message

It is not possible for any human being that God should address him except through inspiration or from behind a veil… or else He sends a messenger who reveals what He wills, by His leave. He is Exalted, All-Wise.

36:20-21 Quality of Messengers

My people, follow the messengers. Follow him who ask you of no reward. These men are guided aright.

25:7 Prophet is Normal and Special

They say: 'What is it with this Messenger who eats food and wanders in the market-place? If only an angel were sent.'

25:31 Enemies of Prophets

Likewise, to every prophet We assigned an enemy from among the criminals. But let your Lord suffice as Guide and Champion.

17:77 God's Original Patterns are Constant

Such was the course among those of Our Messengers We sent before you – and never will you find Our course to vary!

53:9-16 Prophetic Lights

…Until he was two bow-lengths away or even closer. And He revealed to His servant what He revealed. The inner heart did not distort what it saw. Do you then dispute with him what he sees? And certainly, he saw him in another descent, by the lote-tree of the farthest limit near the Garden of Refuge. When that which covers covered the lote-tree…

33:45-46 Prophet's State and Conduct

…We have sent you as a witness, a herald of glad tidings and a warner, and one who calls to God by His leave and a luminous lamp.

39:41 Qur'an, Guidance

We sent down on you the Book for mankind, in truth. Whoever follows guidance does so for the good of his self; whoso strays in error does so to its detriment. You are not their guardian.

C. Prayer & Practice

2:45 Prayers Heavy for the Weak of Faith

Seek help in patience and prayer, prayer that is indeed burdensome except for the devout,

7:205 Remember Diligently

Remember your Lord within yourself, humbly and in awe… And be not among the negligent.

22:77 Prayer and Worship Lead to Contentment

…bend down and prostrate yourselves and worship your Lord…

3:147 Repentance of the Faithful

'Our Lord, forgive us our misdeeds and our excesses. Make us steadfast…'

33:41-43 From Darkness to Light

O you who have attained to faith! Remember God with unceasing remembrance, and glorify Him morning and evening… to lead you out of the darkness and into the light.

13:28 Peaceful Heart

Those who have faith and whose hearts find peace in the remembrance of God, truly it is in the remembrance of God that hearts find peace.

29:45 Necessity of Prayers and God-Awareness

...perform the prayer; prayer forbids indecency and offences. God's remembrance is greater; and God knows the things you work.

87:14-15 Purify the Self and Remembrance of God

He indeed shall be successful who purifies himself and mentions the name of his Lord.

52:48-49 Patience, Praise and Glorifying God

Wait patiently for your Lord's judgement: you are under Our watchful eye. Celebrate the praise of your Lord when you rise. Glorify Him at night and at the fading of the stars.

2:183 Fasting Increases Awareness

Fasting is ordained for you as it was ordained for those before you, so that you might remain cautiously aware.

40:60 Humility and Faith Precedes Prayers

Your Lord says: 'Call upon Me and I shall answer you…'

70:22-28 Prayers, Charity and Trust in the Hereafter

…Those who pray, who are constantly in prayer, who give a rightful share of their wealth, for the beggar and the outcast, who truly believe in the Day of Judgment, and fear the punishment of their Lord – from the punishment of their Lord none can feel secure.

53:60-62 Warning Against Lower Self and Ego

You laugh and do not weep, while you stand with your head held high? Bow down before God and worship.

107:4-5 Religious Rituals without Higher Awareness

So woe to those who pray but are heedless of their prayer.

25:70-73 People of Faith and Loss

Save him who repents, has faith and does good deeds, these God shall replace their sins with favours. And God is All-Forgiving, Compassionate to each… Those who, when reminded of the signs of their Lord, do not bow down, dumb and blind.

D. Towards Full Consciousness

2:207 Giving up the Self in the Way of Allah

And among men is He Who sells himself to seek the pleasure of God…

3:92 Giving up what is Loved Most

None of you will attain virtue unless you give out of what you cherish; whatever you give, Allah knows about it very well.

3:133-136 Preparation for Paradise

Hurry towards your Lord's forgiveness and a Garden as wide as the heavens and earth prepared for the righteous, who give, both in prosperity and adversity, who restrain their anger and pardon people – Allah loves those who do good, who, when they commit indecency or wrong themselves, remember Allah and beg forgiveness for their misdeeds.

5:35 Be Dutiful Seeking Means to Truth

…seek means of nearness to Him and strive hard in His way that you may be successful.

6:153 One Clear Path

And that this is the way leading straight unto Me: follow it, then, and follow not other ways, lest they cause you to deviate from His way. This He has enjoined upon you, so that you might remain cautiously aware.

8:74-75 Life is a Journey Towards Truth

And those who believe, and have emigrated and struggled in the way of God…

15:98-99 True Worship Leads to Awakening

So glorify the praise of your Lord, and be among those who prostrate themselves; and worship your Lord until Certainty comes to you.

22:54 The Straight Path

Let those endowed with knowledge know that it is the Truth from your Lord, and let them believe in it, so that their hearts can find peace therein. God shall surely guide the believers onto a straight path.

17:57 Caution and Desire of Truth

Those they call upon are themselves seeking the means to come to their Lord, which of them shall be nearer; they hope for His mercy, and fear His chastisement. Surely your Lord's chastisement is a thing to beware of.

29:69 Guidance

But those who exerted themselves in Our cause, We shall guide them to Our ways; and God is assuredly with the righteous.

22:35 Conduct on the Path

…who endure whatever happens to them with patience, who keep up the prayer, who give to others out of Our provision to them.

23:8-11 Path of Victory

And those who preserve their trusts and their covenant, who persevere in prayer. Those are the inheritors, who shall inherit Paradise, abiding therein for ever.

37:99 Guidance

He said: 'I shall go to my Lord and He shall guide me.'

37:84 Guidance Due to a Pure Heart

When he came unto his Lord with a pure heart…

20:12 Earthly Abandonment Before Enlightenment

It is Me, your Lord. Remove your sandals. You are in the sacred valley, Tuwa.

73:19 Higher Remembrance

This is a reminder. Let whoever wishes take the way to his Lord.

10:9-10 Guidance

…those who believe, and do deeds of righteousness, their Lord will guide them by their belief; beneath them, rivers flowing in gardens of bliss…

23:57-61 Steadfastness in Spiritual Progress

…Have faith in their Lord's signs… who expend what they expend with hearts anxious for acceptance, knowing that they will surely return to their Lord; are the ones who race toward good deeds and are foremost in them.

50:33 Seekers' Qualification

Who held the Most Gracious in awe, though He is unseen, who comes before Him with a heart turned to Him in devotion.

47:17 Increased Guidance

As for those who are guided, He increases their guidance and causes them to grow in consciousness.

46:19 Levels in Consciousness

For all there are stations, in accordance with their deeds. He will pay them in full for their works, and they shall not be wronged.

87:6-7 Remembrance of God Who Knows All

We shall teach you (the book of truth) and you will not forget.

84:6 Natural Earthly Struggle Towards Source

O Mankind! truly you are toiling laboriously towards your Lord, and will meet Him.

51:50 Prophetic Unison with God

Therefore flee unto God! I am a clear warner from Him to you.

78:39 Day of Reckoning Connects with Now

That is the Day of Truth. So whoever wishes to do so should take the path that leads to his Lord.

56:62 The Origin Lies Within the Soul

You know all about the first creation, will you not remember and reflect?

50:31 Seamless Connection Within Space and Time

And the Garden shall be drawn near to the pious, not far at all.

E. Awakened Being

2:112 When Ego Vanishes the Soul's Perfection Shines

…whoever submits himself entirely to God and is the doer of good, he has his reward from his Lord, and there is no fear for him nor shall he grieve.

3:163 Degrees of Distance from Darkness and Closeness to Light

They are graded in ranks with God, and God sees full well what they do.

3:170 Awakening to the Light of Truth

Happy with what God has given them of His favour; rejoicing that for those they have left behind who have yet to join them there is no fear, nor will they grieve.

3:191 To Reflect and Remember

Those who remember God standing, sitting, and lying down, who reflect on the creation of the heavens and earth (saying): 'Our Lord! You have not created all this without purpose, Glory be to You! Shield us from the torment of the Fire.'

10:25 God's Guidance

Allah calls to the Abode of Peace and guides whomsoever He wills to a path that is straight.

8:2-4 Guided Believers

True believers are those whose hearts tremble with awe when Allah is mentioned, whose faith increases when His signs are recited to them, who put their trust in their Lord, who keep up the prayer and expend of what We provide for them. They are the true believers. High in rank they stand with their Lord, and they shall enjoy His forgiveness and glorious provisions.

21:49 Constant Awareness of God

Those who stand in awe of their Lord, though He is unseen, and who fear the Hour.

7:56 How Signs Are Disclosed to People Who Know

And do not cause corruption and breakdowns on earth after it had been rendered wholesome and do pray and supplicate with fear and good expectation as God's mercy is close to those who do good.

46:13 Belief and Relief

Those who say: 'Our Lord is God,' and are upright. No fear shall come upon them, nor shall they grieve.

25:63-65 Conduct of the Faithful

The servants of the All-Merciful are those who walk in the earth modestly and who, when the ignorant address them, say, 'Peace'; and they who pass the night prostrating themselves before their Lord and standing. Those who say: 'Our Lord, avert from us the torment of hell; its torment is an eternal penalty.'

10:62-64 Victory of the Faithful

Surely the friends of God – no fear shall fall upon them, nor shall they grieve. They who have attained to faith and have always been cautiously aware of Him, to them, glad tidings in this present world, and in the hereafter. There can be no change in the words of God. This indeed is the greatest of triumphs.

9:20 Victory of the Illumined

Those who believe, and have emigrated, and have struggled in the way of God with their possessions and their selves are mightier in rank with God; and those, they are the triumphant...

41:30-31 The Garden is Home of the Awakened

As for those who say 'Our Lord is God' and are upright in deed, angels shall be made to descend upon them: 'Fear not, and do not grieve. Here are glad tidings of the Garden which you were promised. We are your guardians in this life and the next. In it you shall have all that your selves desire, all that you pray for.'

66:8 Abode of the Garden

Believers, turn to Allah in sincere repentance. Your Lord may well cancel your bad deeds for you and admit you into gardens graced with flowing streams, on a day when Allah will not disgrace the Prophet or those who have believed with him. With their lights streaming out ahead of them and to their right, they will say, 'Lord, perfect our lights for us and forgive us: You have power over everything.'

32:15-16 Conduct of Believers

Truly they believe in Our signs who, when reminded of them, fall in prostration, glorifying the praise of their Lord; nor are they too proud to do so. Their sides shun their couches as they call on their Lord in fear and hope; and they expend what We have provided them.

56:8-12 Three Ranks of Humans

The companions of the Right; what are the companions of the Right! The companions of the Left; what are the companions of the Left! And those in front, ahead indeed! These shall be the nearest, in the Gardens of Bliss.

83:20-24 Abode of the Awakened

A Book written, witnessed by those brought near. Most surely the righteous shall be in bliss, seated on couches, gazing around. You will recognize on their faces the radiance of bliss.

9:88-89 Sacrifice and Dedicated Actions

But the Messenger and the believers with him have laboured hard with their properties and persons. To them belong the finest rewards. These shall truly gain success. God has prepared for them gardens underneath which rivers flow, therein to dwell forever; that is the mighty triumph.

89:27-30 Self Awakening to Soul and its Garden

O Self at peace! Return to your Lord, well pleased, well pleasing, and enter among My worshippers, and enter My Garden!

F.   Teachers, Mirrors & Reflectors of Truth

3:159 Prophetic Conduct

By an act of mercy from God, you were gentle in your dealings with them – had you been harsh, or hard-hearted, they would have dispersed and left you, so pardon them and ask forgiveness for them. Consult with them about matters, then, when you have decided on a course of action, put your trust in God. God loves those who put their trust in Him.

5:105 Caution and Care of the Lower Self

O you who believe! Take care of your selves; He Who errs cannot hurt you when you are on the right way; to God is the return of all, and He will inform you of what you did.

6:107 Human Effort Needed for Illumination

Had God willed, they would not have worshipped idols. But We did not appoint you their keeper, nor are you their guardian.

4:80 Obedience to God and the Messenger

Whoever obeys the Messenger obeys God and whoever turns away, We have not sent you to be their keeper.

10:99 Faith Cannot be Forced

Had your Lord willed it, all on earth, every single one, would have believed. Will you then compel people to become believers?

16:75 Metaphor of Guidance and Loss

God strikes a simile: a bonded slave who has no power over anything, and a person whom We granted a goodly provision, from which he expends in secret and in the open. Are these two equal? Praise be to God! But most of them have no knowledge.

8:62-64 Connections of Hearts to a Divine Power

Had you spent all that is on earth you could not have brought their hearts together, but it was God Who reconciled them to one another. He is Almighty, All-Wise. O Prophet, God is sufficient for you and the believers who have followed you.

7:188 Limits of Human Ability

Say: 'I have no power to do myself good or harm save as God wills. Had I known the Unseen I would have done myself much good, and no harm would have touched me. I am merely a Warner, and a herald of good tidings to a people who believe.'

27:79-81 Most Are Blind and Deaf

Put your trust in God, for you are upon a manifest truth. You cannot make the dead hear, nor make the deaf hear the call if they turn their backs and depart. You shall not guide the blind out of their error neither shalt thou make any to hear, save such as believe in Our signs, and so surrender.

28:56 God Guides Who is Ready

You cannot guide those whom you love; rather, Allah guides whom He wishes, and He knows best who are guided aright.

25:30 Warning Regarding the Abandonment of the Qur'an

The Messenger shall say: 'My Lord, what is wrong with my people who have abandoned this Qur'an.'

31:23 Those in Denial Will Eventually Discover Their Error

And whoever disbelieves, do not let his disbelief grieve you; to Us is their return, then We will inform them of what they did. Surely God is the Knower of what is in the hearts.

27:92 Guidance Without Coercion

...Whoever is guided, is guided for his own good. Whoso strays into error, say: 'I am merely a warner.'

26:3 Limits of Empathy and Desire to Help Others

And you are not to torture yourself because they are not believers.

63:4 Outwardly Impressive Beings but Dead at Heart

When you see them, you are impressed by their outward appearance, and when they speak, you listen to their words. But they are like wooden stilts: they suppose that every shout is against them. So be on your guard against them. May God strike them down! How they pervert the truth.

39:17-19 To Do One's Best Always, the Soul is Ever Perfect

...So announce glad tidings to My servants, who listen to what is said and follow what is best. These are the ones God has guided; they who are the possessors of intellect. As for him who deserves the decree of punishment, is it you who can save those in the Fire?

46:35 Steadfastness Needed with Those of Weak Faith

So, remain steadfast as other resolute messengers had stood fast. Do not be impatient with them. It will be as if, when they witness the Day they are promised, they had been on earth a mere hour of a day. That is the message! Will any be destroyed but the dissolute?

41:6 Outer Sameness with Inner Distinction

Say: 'I am but a human being like you, to whom inspiration is sent. Your God is in truth One God. Act righteously in His sight and seek His forgiveness. And woe to the polytheists.'

49:17 Islam and Submission to God are His Gifts

They count it as a favour to you that they have accepted Islam. Say, 'Do not count your submission as a favour to me. No, rather God confers a favour on you, in that He has guided you to belief if you are truthful.'

51:55 Reminding Benefits the Believers

And remind, reminding is good for the believers.

88:21-22 Prophetic Message is to Remind

Therefore, do remind, for you are only a reminder, you are not there to control them.

18:67-68 Patience is Natural Due to Knowledge

He said: 'Assuredly you will not be able to bear with me patiently. And how would you bear patiently what you have not encompassed in knowledge?'

38:86-88 Messenger's Reward is the Light of the Heart

Say, 'I ask no reward from you for this, nor do I claim to be what I am not: this is but a Remembrance to mankind. In time you will certainly come to know its truth.'

42:15 Perfect Reading of Reality

And say: 'I believe in whatever Book Allah has sent down; I have been commanded to be just between you. Allah is our Lord and your Lord. We have our deeds, and you have your deeds; there is no argument between us and you; Allah shall bring us together, and unto Him is the homecoming.'

About the Author

Born in Karbala, Iraq, Shaykh Fadhlalla Haeri, comes from severalgenerations of religious and spiritual leaders. After several years living and working in the west, he rediscovered the universal relevance of the Qur'an and Islamic teachings for our present day. His emphasis has been on transformative worship and refi nement of conduct, as preludes to the realisation of the prevalence of Divine Grace. He considers that the purpose of life is to know and resonate with the eternal essence of the one and only Lifegiver—Allah

CPSIA information can be obtained
at www.ICGtesting.com
Printed in the USA
LVHW021041100122
708185LV00015B/2206

9 781928 329211